THE MYSTERIOUS PARABLE

A LITERARY STUDY

BY

MADELEINE BOUCHER

Department of Theology

Fordham University

The Catholic Biblical Association of America

Washington, D.C. 20064

1977

THE MYSTERIOUS PARABLE
A Literary Study
by Madeleine Boucher

© 1977 The Catholic Biblical Association of America
Washington, D.C.

PRODUCED IN THE UNITED STATES

Grateful acknowledgment is made for permission to quote from the following work:

The Babylonian Talmud (ed. Isadore Epstein; 34 vols.; London: Soncino Press, 1935–48), Berakoth (tr. Maurice Simon). Used by permission of Soncino Press, London, England.

Biblical quotations are from the Revised Standard Version.

Library of Congress Cataloging in Publication Data

Boucher, Madeleine, 1936–
  The mysterious parable.

  (The Catholic Biblical quarterly: Monograph series; 6)
  Bibliography: p.
  Includes indexes.
  1. Jesus Christ—Parables. I. Title. II. Series.
BT375.2.B64   226'.8'066   76-51260
ISBN 0-915170-05-1

THE CATHOLIC BIBLICAL QUARTERLY

MONOGRAPH SERIES

6

THE MYSTERIOUS PARABLE

A LITERARY STUDY

by

Madeleine Boucher

TO MY MOTHER

Table of Contents

Biblical quotations are from the Revised Standard Version.

Abbreviations Employed for the Qumran Literature

CD	Cairo-Damascus Document
1QH	*Hôdāyôt* (Hymns of Thanksgiving)
1QpHab	Pesher (Commentary) on Habakkuk
1QM	*Milḥāmâ* (War Scroll)
1QS	*Serek hayyaḥad* (Rule of the Community; Manual of Discipline)
1QSa	Rule of the Congregation (Appendix A to 1QS)

PREFACE

This work, a revision of my doctoral dissertation at Brown University, was completed with the indispensable aid of scholars in the fields of both biblical and literary studies.

On the biblical side, I am exceedingly grateful to my dissertation advisor, Professor William R. Schoedel of the University of Illinois, for his guidance throughout this project, and indeed throughout my graduate studies in religion. I would like also to thank his colleague, Professor Vernon K. Robbins, for bringing a number of works and issues to my attention; and the other members of my dissertation committee, Professors Horst R. Moehring and Ernest S. Frerichs of Brown University, for their kind help and encouragement.

On the literary side, I am deeply grateful to the literary theorist, Professor J. Craig La Drière of Harvard University, who taught me literary theory and criticism during my studies for the M.A. in English, and who offered many valuable suggestions during the various stages of preparation of this book.

I wish to express heartfelt thanks also to my sister Pauline who, as a librarian, generously gave me expert assistance in bibliographical matters.

The shortcomings of the study are, however, attributable only to me.

INTRODUCTION

Bultmann once wrote the following request in the course of defending Jülicher's extraordinarily influential theory on the parables of Jesus: "Most of all we must ask of Juelicher's critics a clarity of concept, and whether this be understood in Aristotelian or other terms is not a matter of fundamental significance."[1] The present study is an attempt to respond to this fair and no doubt friendly challenge, for I find myself a radical critic of Jülicher's theory. It is my view that the study of the parables is still burdened with problems, and that these will not be resolved so long as certain misunderstandings, either an element of or a result of Jülicher's theory, continue to be entertained. Perhaps the most basic of these errors, as this study is in part intended to demonstrate, is Jülicher's assertion that the parables are not allegories.

The problems are almost all literary problems, and so nothing is more needed in the discussion than the introduction of certain concepts from literary theory. But the theory must be sound, and it must be properly used. The error of Jülicher and others is not that they have employed tools taken from classical rhetoric for the analysis of Semitic parables, as has sometimes been said. On the contrary, the use of both ancient and modern western literary theory in the analysis of literary works of any culture is not only valid but illuminating. If, however, the analyst's conceptual scheme is flawed by incorrect definitions and distinctions, the results cannot but be incorrect. It is in a faulty theoretical framework that the error of Jülicher lies. What follows is an attempt to provide a corrective to misconceptions about the parable by means of more accurate definitions and distinctions.

This study should not, however, be taken as a mere exercise in exchanging one arbitrary definition for another. The central object of interest in the discussion is the literary phenomena themselves, especially those structures which we conventionally call allegory and parable. It will not do to begin by composing a definition of allegory and parable and then to regard as allegory or parable only those examples to which one's *a priori* definition apply, thus attempting to bend the phenomena to fit the definition. The starting-point must be the literary structures themselves. The only sound method is to begin by observing a number of examples of the same recurrent phenomenon, that is, examples of those constructs which it is generally agreed belong to the same class, and then to derive the definition of the phenomenon from those examples. A definition is sound or not depending solely on whether it correctly describes the thing—what it is (material and

---

1. Rudolf Bultmann, *The History of the Synoptic Tradition* (tr. John Marsh from 4th German ed.; New York: Harper & Row, 1963 [1st German ed., 1921]) 198.

structure) and what it does (function). The description, like the classification and observation, must be *accurate*, *precise*, and *consistent* if it is to be scientific. What is at stake, then, is a correct description and hence a correct understanding of the literary artifacts, namely the Synoptic parables.

The threefold goal of this study is, first, to provide a sound definition and description of the parable as a verbal construct, since a clear understanding of the parable is desirable in itself; second, to provide a definition which will, moreover, explain how it was possible for the parable to be understood (quite rightly) as mysterious speech in the Semitic tradition; and third, to show how the parable could be the starting-point for the Markan theology of mystery.

The study is primarily a literary one. Such study of the Bible is still in the beginning stages. Until recently, literary work has perhaps seemed somewhat unimportant to those who by temperament or training are inclined toward historical or theological work. But the Bible is, after all, literature. The biblical books, and their component parts such as the parables, are literary constructs. The literary analysis of the Bible, then, needs no further justification.

The literary theorist, the historian, and the theologian may all look at the same object—say the parable—but they will examine different aspects of it. A parable is a verbal artifact, that is, a structure composed of sound and meaning. The literary theorist will be most interested in the aspect of structuredness; he will seek to determine what kind of construct a parable is, how it is put together. The main (though not the sole) object of his interest will be *structure of meaning*. The historian and the theologian will be more interested in the *meaning* itself, seeking to determine what the parable, or the interpretation appended to it, says. They will relate the meaning to a wider context—the historian perhaps to the history of the Synoptic tradition or to the history of early Christian thought, the theologian perhaps to a system of eschatology or ethics. There is no question that the literary theorist can make a contribution to the knowledge of parables equal in value to that of the historian or theologian. One could even argue that literary analysis is, in biblical studies, basic to historical and theological discourse. The exegete will make sounder historical and theological statements about the parable if he understands it clearly as a verbal construct—as perhaps the present study will show.

VIEWS AND COUNTERVIEWS ON THE PARABLE

It seems to be a widely held assumption that the most basic problems on parables have been solved since the late nineteenth century, and that only peripheral matters remain to be worked out. This supposition falls rather short of the truth; in fact, it is the most crucial issues that remain to be resolved. The following survey of the research from Jülicher down to the present is intended, not to give a comprehensive account, but simply to bring these issues into the sharpest possible focus.

A. JÜLICHER

It was Jülicher, of course, who proposed the classification of the parables which has remained standard in the scholarly literature.[1] He placed the majority of the parables in two classes: the *similitude* (*Gleichnis*) and the *parable* in the narrow sense (*Parabel*). Both compare something in the religious domain to something in another domain. Yet they are distinct. The similitude narrates a typical or recurrent event in real life, usually in the present tense (e.g., the seed growing by itself, Mk 4:26–29; the lost sheep and the lost coin, Mt 18:12–14; Lk 15:3–10). The parable tells a fictitious story, or narrates one particular incident which is invented, usually in the past tense (e.g., the workers in the vineyard, Mt 20:1–16; the prodigal son, Lk 15:11–32). According to Jülicher, the Synoptic *similitude* belongs to the same class as Aristotle's *parabolē* (and Quintilian's *similitudo*)[2] and the Synoptic *parable* to the same class as Aristotle's *logos* or fable (and Quintilian's *fabella* or *fabula*).[3] (See Appendix for the use of the terms in the classical literature.)

In addition, Jülicher distinguished four parables, all Lukan, to which he gave the name *exemplary story* (*Beispielerzählung*: the good Samaritan, Lk 10:29–37; the rich fool, Lk 12:16–21; the rich man and Lazarus, Lk 16:19–31; the Pharisee and the tax collector, Lk 18:9–14). This type differs from the first two in that it presents, not a comparison, but an example to be imitated.

What is most important in Jülicher's work is the explanation he proposed

---

1. Adolf Jülicher, *Die Gleichnisreden Jesu*: I. *Die Gleichnisreden Jesu im Allgemeinen*; II. *Auslegung der Gleichnisreden der drei ersten Evangelien* (Tübingen: Mohr; I, 2nd ed., 1899 [1st ed., 1886]; II, 2nd ed., 1910 [1st ed., 1899]). The classification of parables is discussed in Vol. I: similitude, pp. 58–80; parable, pp. 92–111; exemplary story, pp. 112–15.

2. Jülicher, *Gleichnisreden* I, 69.

3. Jülicher, *Gleichnisreden* I, 98.

for the notion, stated explicitly in the Gospel of Mark, that parables are mysterious speech. He based his explanation on a theory which sharply differentiates between parable and allegory; this, too, has remained the standard explanation in the scholarly literature—despite the fact that it is surely not correct.

In constructing his theory, Jülicher began with the simile and metaphor, which he described as two radically distinct devices of speech.[4] He used the example given by Aristotle: to say "Achilles rushed on like a lion" is a simile; but to say of Achilles "A lion rushed on" is a metaphor (*Rhetoric* III.3.4). In a simile the two things being compared are explicitly named and the two words are set side by side, so that there can be no error in interpretation. The simile is therefore always clear. In a metaphor, on the other hand, one word is substituted for another and of the two things being compared only one is explicitly named, so that the hearer must know what the missing word is in order to grasp the meaning; he must know, for example, that the word "lion" stands for "Achilles." Therefore every metaphor, at least out of context, is a mystery. The words in a simile are to be taken literally, for they mean what they say; the words in a metaphor are not to be taken literally, for they say one thing and mean another. The simile requires no explanation; the metaphor must be deciphered.

Now, what is true of the simile is true of the parable, for a *parable*, says Jülicher, is *an extended simile*. And what is true of the metaphor is true of the allegory, for an *allegory*, according to Jülicher, is composed of *a series of metaphors*.[5] The parable is literal speech; it designates the two things it is comparing, and requires no explanation. The allegory is metaphorical speech; it involves a substitution, and must be decoded. The parable illuminates and instructs; the allegory disguises a thing.

It is important to note the precise formulation of Jülicher's definition of allegory; it is made up of *many* metaphors. He chose, he said, to restrict his definition to that of Cicero, who wrote: "When there is a continuous stream of metaphors, a wholly different style of speech (*alia oratio*) is produced; consequently the Greeks call it *allēgoria* or 'allegory'" (*Orator* 27.94).[6] That is to say, the allegory has as many points of comparison as it has metaphors. The parable, on the other hand, has but one point of comparison; the hearer should take from it a single thought, which was always, for Jülicher, a general, universally applicable, religious or moral principle.[7]

Jülicher was firmly convinced that Jesus could have taught only in parables, and never in allegories, since his purpose undoubtedly was to instruct the simple people of the land; he would not have used speech that

---

4. Jülicher gives his description of simile and metaphor in *Gleichnisreden* I, 52–58.

5. Jülicher discusses the distinction between parable and allegory in *Gleichnisreden* I, 58–80.

6. Jülicher, *Gleichnisreden* I, 51. The translation is from the Loeb Classical Library edition of Cicero *Brutus; Orator* (tr. H. M. Hubbell; Cambridge: Harvard University Press, 1962).

7. Jülicher, *Gleichnisreden* I, 74.

was inscrutable. Before they came into the hands of redactors, Jülicher believed, all the parables—*similitudes, parables*, and *exemplary stories*— were literal speech (*eigentliche Rede*). The evangelists, however, mistook them for allegories, for non-literal speech, and presented them so in the Gospels.[8]

The understanding—or, Jülicher would say, misunderstanding—of the evangelists is expressed most strikingly in Mark 4, where Jesus says, in reply to the disciples' question in private "concerning the parables" (vs. 10):

> To you has been given the secret of the kingdom of God, but for those outside everything is in parables; so that (*hina*) *they may indeed see but not perceive, and may indeed hear but not understand; lest (mēpote) they should turn again, and be forgiven.*
>
> (vss. 11–12; adaptation of Isa 6:9–10)

Thus a theory of the parables as mysterious speech is combined with a theory of predestination to produce a very hard saying indeed, one which taken as it stands can hardly be attributed to Jesus.[9]

In addition, according to Jülicher's scheme at least two Synoptic parables are allegories (the wicked tenants, Mk 12:1–11; Mt 21:33–45; Lk 20:9–18; and the Matthean version of the marriage feast, Mt 22:1–14; cf. Lk 14: 16–24); they cannot, therefore, be authentic parables of Jesus. Moreover, there are secondary, i.e., allegorical or point-by-point, interpretations appended to a number of parables, the most notorious being the interpretation of the parable of the sower, also found in Mark 4. Nor did this kind of tampering end with the writing of the Gospels; it has gone on in the history of the Church even to the present time, whenever preachers and writers of commentaries have interpreted the parables metaphorically, making them say things Jesus never intended. This proliferation of interpretations is the result of a general failure to realize that parables are not allegories.[10]

B. CRITICISMS OF JÜLICHER'S THEORY

Reactions to Jülicher's thesis have not been wanting. Almost immediately scholars questioned his method of analyzing the Synoptic parables with concepts borrowed from classical rhetoric; they insisted that the parables be viewed as part of the tradition of the Semitic *māšāl* which, they held, included allegories as well as parables, since the Hebrew mind made no distinction between the two. They observed that in the biblical and related literatures the word *māšāl* had always referred to a much wider variety of sayings than Jülicher's three classes. (See Appendix for the uses of the term *māšāl* in the biblical and rabbinic literatures.)

8. Jülicher, *Gleichnisreden* I, 49.
9. Jülicher, *Gleichnisreden* I, 118–48.
10. See Jülicher's "Geschichte der Auslegung der Gleichnisreden Jesu," *Gleichnisreden* I, 203–322.

Fiebig, in his two major studies of the rabbinic *mᵉšālîm*,[11] the closest in time and place to those of Jesus, showed that they contained many metaphors, some of them standard. He divided the *mᵉšālîm* into what he called pure parables, pure allegories, and mixed parable-allegories, depending on how many metaphors were to be found in them. He also noted that the rabbinic *māšāl* often had to be followed by an interpretation.

Lagrange[12] paid special attention to the problem of mysteriousness. He pointed out that in the OT and Jewish writings there appear a number of explicit references to the *māšāl* as mysterious, which show this notion to be an ancient and traditional one.[13] Lagrange attributed this understanding of the *māšāl* to the kind of speech it is: its purpose is to strike the imagination, to pique the curiousity of the listener, to make him work to arrive at the meaning, but only so that the lesson will be more deeply engraved on his mind.

T. W. Manson[14] suggested that the obvious place to begin a study of the Synoptic parables is not with western treatises on rhetoric but with the OT. It is there that he, too, found the answer to the problem of mysteriousness. His theory depends on a distinction between the meaning and the application of a parable. The hearer, he believed, might understand perfectly the parable's meaning, while failing to grasp its application altogether (as in Nathan's ewe lamb, 2 Sam 12:1-7).

Hermaniuk[15] put forward an explanation for the parable's mysteriousness which differs greatly from that of Lagrange and Manson. He proposed distinct definitions for the Semitic *māšāl* on the one hand and the Greek *parabolē* and *logos* on the other. Having examined the occurrences of the word *māšāl* in the OT and Jewish literature, he concluded that it did not originally mean a comparison at all, but first a symbol, then a prophetic and eventually an apocalyptic oracle, a medium for revealing heavenly and eschatological secrets.[16] He supported this definition with two observations. First, the aspect of comparison is found in few of the OT and Intertestamental speeches which are explicitly called *māšāl*. Second, the term *māšāl* is conspicuously missing from those OT narratives which are without question comparisons and which most resemble the Synoptic parables (Jgs 9:7-20; 2 Sam 12:1-7; 14:5-13; 1 Kgs 20:39-42; 2 Kgs 14:9-10; Isa 5:1-7; 28:23-29;

11. Paul Fiebig, *Altjüdische Gleichnisse und die Gleichnisse Jesu* (Tübingen: Mohr, 1904); *Die Gleichnisreden Jesu im Lichte der rabbinischen Gleichnisse des neutestamentlichen Zeitalters* (Tübingen: Mohr, 1912).

12. M.-J. Lagrange, "La parabole en dehors de l'Evangile," *RB* 2/6 (1909) 198–212, 342–67.

13. See Ezek 17:2; Hab 2:6; Pss 49:5 (LXX 48:5; RSV 49:4); 78:2 (LXX 77:2); Prov 1:5b–6; Sir 39:2–3; 47:15 (in the Greek); 47:17 (in the Hebrew); *1 Enoch* 68:1; see also 2 Sam 12:1–7; 14:5–13; 1 Kgs 20:39–42.

14. T. W. Manson, *The Teaching of Jesus: Studies of Its Form and Content* (1st paperback ed.; Cambridge: Cambridge University Press, 1963 [1st ed., 1931]) 57–81, esp. 64–66.

15. Maxime Hermaniuk, *La parabole évangélique* (Louvain: Bibliotheca Alfonsiana, 1947).

16. Hermaniuk, *La parabole*, 62–153, esp. 123–24, 153.

Ezek 19:1–9,10–14).[17] (See Appendix.) It was only in late Judaism that there entered into the rabbinic tradition the Greek "parable," which Hermaniuk defined as a comparison intended to clarify a thing.[18] Thus, again, the Semitic *māšāl* was obscure, the Greek "parable" clear.

Hermaniuk then posed the question whether the NT parables are related to the Semitic, or to a rabbinic adaptation of the Greek type.[19] He answered by distinguishing between the "form" and "content" of the Synoptic parables. In "form" all of the NT parables—which he classified as *similitude, parable, allegory, mixed type, exemplary story, proverb*—are descended from the Greek tradition, not directly, but as mediated by the rabbis.[20] In "content," however, they are descended from the OT and apocalyptic tradition, since they are revelations of the mystery of the kingdom of God.[21]

The goal of the line of inquiry pursued by these four scholars was, of course, to show that the view of the parable as mysterious was not an invention of the first generation of Christians, but that it probably reflected the mind of Jesus, who was following a tradition known to all Palestinian Jews.

Other scholars have studied the Synoptic parables themselves and argued the same point. Black[22] asserted that there are no *a priori* reasons why Jesus should not have taught sometimes in allegory; the difference between parable and allegory is one of degree, not kind. Brown,[23] too, challenged the assumption that Jesus ever distinguished between parable and allegory. Gerhardsson,[24] in an article on the parable of the sower, held that the parable and the interpretation suit each other perfectly; either both are authentic, or both are secondary. Baird[25] pointed out that in the Synoptic Gospels roughly twice the number of parables are explained to the disciples as to the non-disciples, and twice the number are left unexplained to the non-disciples as to the disciples—a consistency which, he submitted, reflects the historical reality.

This is not an exhaustive, but a representative list of works that take issue with Jülicher's thesis. What is most interesting to note is that all of them, however critical they may be of Jülicher's theory, accept his definition of parable and allegory. Yet it is just at this fundamental point that Jülicher

17. Hermaniuk, *La parabole*, 115–20.
18. Hermaniuk, *La parabole*, 153–89, esp. 157–58.
19. Hermaniuk, *La parabole*, 194.
20. Hermaniuk, *La parabole*, 194–264, esp. 263–64.
21. Hermaniuk, *La parabole*, 264–301, esp. 301.
22. Matthew Black, "The Parables as Allegory," *BJRL* 42 (1959–60) 273–87.
23. Raymond E. Brown, Ch. 13: "Parable and Allegory Reconsidered," *New Testament Essays* (Milwaukee, Wis.: Bruce, 1965) 254–64. (A reprint of the article in *NovT* 5 [1962] 36–45.)
24. Birger Gerhardsson, "The Parable of the Sower and Its Interpretation" (tr. John Toy), *NTS* 14 (1967–68) 165–93.
25. J. Arthur Baird, "A Pragmatic Approach to Parable Exegesis: Some New Evidence on Mark 4.11,33–34," *JBL* 76 (1957) 201–207.

made his misleading error; and so the criticisms, many of which are sound, are nevertheless not radical enough. Still, the influence of these works has been felt, and has resulted in some modification, though hardly a general rejection, of Jülicher's theory.

C. MODIFICATIONS OF JÜLICHER'S THEORY

Most scholars of the parables have accepted the evidence presented by Fiebig that parables contain metaphors; at the same time, they still hold to Jülicher's axiom that parables are not allegories. The two views have been yoked together by Bultmann,[26] Hauck,[27] and Via,[28] for example. Typical is Bultmann's assertion: allegory is intended to disguise something, while a parable is not; so what Fiebig adduced as allegorical features in the rabbinic parables are really not allegory at all, but merely stock metaphors, for God as king, for man as servant, and the like.

Some scholars have expressed the opinion that the parables are not quite so clear as Jülicher had maintained; at the same time, they still insist with Jülicher that the purpose of a parable is to illuminate. Again the two views have been pulled together by Hauck[29] and Via,[30] for example. Via has stated this position quite simply: it is contrary to the nature of a parable that it could be intended to conceal its meaning; yet the meaning of a parable is not always plain.

It might be said at this point that the ambiguity evident in these statements seems to indicate that there is something quite amiss in Jülicher's theory which sets over against each other the lucid parable, an extended simile, and the dark allegory, a sequence of metaphors.

Finally, other scholars, notably Cadoux,[31] Dodd,[32] Jeremias,[33] and Linnemann,[34] have modified Jülicher's theory in another respect, putting forward the view that the parables of Jesus were intended not to teach some general religious or ethical truth applicable in all times, but to proclaim the coming of the kingdom of God. The exegete must set each parable in the

---

26. Bultmann, *Synoptic Tradition*, 198.

27. Friedrich Hauck, "*Parabolē*," *TDNT* V, 752–53.

28. Dan Otto Via Jr., *The Parables: Their Literary and Existential Dimension* (Philadelphia: Fortress Press, 1967) 14–15.

29. Hauck, "*Parabolē*," 756.

30. Via, *Parables*, 10.

31. A. T. Cadoux, *The Parables of Jesus: Their Art and Use* (London: Clarke, 1930).

32. C. H. Dodd, *The Parables of the Kingdom* (rev. ed.; New York: Scribner's, 1961 [1st ed., 1935]).

33. Joachim Jeremias, *The Parables of Jesus* (rev. ed.; tr. S. H. Hooke from 6th German ed.; New York: Scribner's, 1963 [1st German ed., 1947]).

34. Eta Linnemann, *Jesus of the Parables* (tr. John Sturdy from 3rd German ed.; New York: Harper & Row, 1966 [1st German ed., 1961]).

ministry of Jesus, that is, must attempt to reconstruct the specific situation in which a parable was first uttered, and to ascertain as precisely as possible the thoughts and values of both Jesus and his audience, in order correctly to interpret it.

Recently Via,[35] while continuing in the tradition of Jülicher, has examined the parables specifically as works of literature. According to Via, the basic difference between parable and allegory is that the parable has coherence of structure which the allegory lacks. The elements in a parable are related primarily to one another, the elements in an allegory primarily to the outside world. This means that the parable is aesthetic, the allegory is not—for what constitutes the aesthetic is precisely coherence of structure.[36] The assertion that parables are aesthetic constructs or literature may be said to be the core of Via's thesis. It is important to note that he uses the terms "aesthetic speech" and "literature" interchangeably.[37]

Via then discusses the view held by some literary theorists, especially the new critics, that works of literature are "autonomous," to use his term. This is the view that a literary work is independent of the author, of the reader, of philosophical and theological thought, and of society. It warns against the error of seeking the meaning of a work in the author's intention (the "intentional fallacy") and against the error of confusing the value of a work with its psychological effects in the reader (the "affective fallacy"). This view is summarized by saying that art is autotelic, an end in itself rather than a means—a view which Via accepts with moderate reservations.[38]

Via insists that, because the parables are, within limits, "autonomous" works, they can and should be detached from their setting in the ministry of Jesus. He is critical of the historical approach of Dodd, Jeremias, and others, partly because it is difficult to ascertain the original meaning of a parable, partly because it may leave the parable with little if anything to say to the present.[39] The best interpretation is an existential, secular, non-allegorical one, which understands the parable as a statement about human interrelationships, and which thus brings out its permanently relevant meaning. Because the parable presents this statement aesthetically, it has the power to compel the hearer to decision, and thus it becomes an "event."[40]

It should be evident from a review of the research such as this one that not only peripheral, but quite central problems, still remain to be solved. These, it may be urged, include such questions as the following: how accurately to trace the provenance of the Synoptic parables; what it means to say that the

35. Via, *Parables*.
36. Via, *Parables*, 24–25.
37. For example, on p. 74.
38. Via, *Parables*, 77–88.
39. Via, *Parables*, 21–24.
40. Via, *Parables*, 88–107.

parables are literature; how to define parable and allegory correctly and in such a way as to explain satisfactorily why the parables were understood by the ancients as mysterious; and whether to interpret the parables in keeping with their historical context or in a manner more relevant to the present. The answers to these questions, insofar as they can be attained, will result in a fairly clear comprehension of the parable as a verbal construct.

2

THE PARABLE AS A LITERARY CLASS

The task at hand is to bring forward some theoretical concepts that will illuminate the parable as a literary class. Those presented here employ standard definitions available in classical and contemporary literary handbooks and familiar to all students of literature;[1] but they are drawn especially from the work of Professor J. Craig La Drière, whose literary theory always proves invaluable in the solution of problems like those encountered in the study of the parables.[2]

A. THE PROVENANCE OF THE SYNOPTIC PARABLES

In the assessment of Hermaniuk's thesis, perhaps the most basic criticism that must be made is that he has confounded what are really two separate topics. One is the history of the term *māšāl/parabolē*, the other the history of certain literary classes. A history of the term is in itself interesting; but it does not tell us anything about the origins of the Synoptic speeches. Only the history of the literary classes can provide an answer to that question. How

1. Especially useful for classical rhetoric are the Loeb Classical Library editions of the following works: Aristotle *The "Art" of Rhetoric* (tr. John Henry Freese; Cambridge: Harvard University Press, 1926); Cicero *Orator* (tr. H. M. Hubbell; Cambridge: Harvard University Press, 1962); Quintilian *The Institutio Oratoria of Quintilian* (tr. H. E. Butler; 4 vols.; Cambridge: Harvard University Press, 1920–22). Quotations from these works in the present study follow the translations of the Loeb Classical Library editions, except where an occasional key term is translated differently.

The best modern handbooks of rhetorical terms are Heinrich Lausberg, *Handbuch der literarischen Rhetorik: Eine Grundlegung der Literaturwissenschaft* (2 vols.; Munich: Hueber, 1960); Henri Morier, *Dictionnaire de poétique et de rhétorique* (Paris: Presses Universitaires de France, 1961); and Richard A. Lanham, *A Handlist of Rhetorical Terms: A Guide for Students of English Literature* (Berkeley: University of California Press, 1968).

Also helpful are these dictionaries: Joseph T. Shipley, ed., *Dictionary of World Literary Terms* (rev., enl. ed.; Boston: The Writer, 1970); and C. Hugh Holman, *A Handbook to Literature* (based on original by William Flint Thrall and Addison Hibbard; 3rd ed.; New York: Odyssey Press, 1972).

2. See especially the following articles by La Drière: "Rhetoric and 'Merely Verbal' Art," in *English Institute Essays 1948* (ed. D. A. Robertson Jr.; New York: AMS Press, 1965) 123–52; "Structure, Sound, and Meaning," in *English Institute Essays 1956. Sound and Poetry* (ed. Northrop Frye; New York: Columbia University Press, 1957) 85–108; "Literary Form and Form in the Other Arts," in *Stil- und Formprobleme in der Literatur* (ed. Paul Böckmann; Heidelberg: Winter, 1959) 28–37; and his articles, "Classification, Literary," and "Form," in Shipley, ed., *Dictionary of World Literary Terms*. Scholars interested in pursuing topics related to problems of form and genre in biblical writings would find these essays an excellent starting point.

11

and when these speeches came to be called *māšāl* and *parabolē* is irrelevant, for the simple reason that a similitude or parable by any other name is still a similitude or parable.

Having decided that the OT speeches that compare one thing to another are not m^e*šālîm/parabolai*, since they do not bear the name, Hermaniuk excludes them, or at least appears to, from his history of the literary classes. Then, observing that some of the rabbinic and NT m^e*šālîm/parabolai* are themselves speeches which compare one thing to another, he must appeal to the Greek literature to explain their origin. It is difficult to tell whether Hermaniuk really means that with the hellenization of the east the "Greek parable," that is, the parable as comparison, first made its appearance in Jewish (oral and written) literature. That appears to be what he says; but he may mean only that the similitude and parable, which had for centuries existed in the Semitic tradition, were first given the name *māšāl* at this period, because the word *māšāl*, having been translated *parabolē* in the LXX, now came to mean, for the first time, comparison. The latter may be a defensible thesis; the former is not, since examples of these literary classes occur in some of the early books of the OT, and certainly did not first enter into Jewish literature in the Hellenistic period.

The solution to the central problem, that of the provenance of the Synoptic speeches, can and should be found quite apart from any linguistic considerations. All that is needed is to note the examples of the literary classes in question which occur—by whatever name—in the OT. Every kind of speech called *parabolē* in the NT appears also in the OT (though not every kind of speech called *māšāl* in the OT appears in the NT). Following are examples of speeches designated as *parabolai* in the Synoptic Gospels, each of which is followed by a corresponding example from the OT. The list is not an attempt to classify the *parabolai*, but only to show that they are of Semitic, not Greek, provenance. The comparisons, it should be noted, are based on form or structure, not on meaning.

Synoptic proverbs such as "Physician, heal yourself" (Lk 4:23); "And if a blind man leads a blind man, both will fall into a pit" (Mt 15:14; Lk 6:39) are certainly descended from those in the OT (e.g., 1 Sam 24:13 [LXX 24:14]; Ezek 16:44).

The Synoptic wisdom sayings, most of which are composed of two parallel members (e.g., Mk 7:15; Mt 15:11; Mt 7:11; Lk 11:13), are quite like those in the OT, especially the wisdom books (e.g., Prov 26:20; Sir 22:16). Those composed of three parallel members (e.g., Mk 3:24–26; Mt 12:25–26; Lk 11:17–18) also have their counterpart in the OT wisdom books (e.g., Prov 6:27–29).[3]

3. On the wisdom sayings in the NT, see C. F. Burney, *The Poetry of Our Lord: An Examination of the Formal Elements of Hebrew Poetry in the Discourses of Jesus Christ* (Oxford: Clarendon Press, 1925).

A similitude such as that of the mustard seed (Mk 4:30–32; Mt 13:31–32; Lk 13:18–19) has its ancestor in a prophetic book (Ezek 31:2–6). Another type of similitude, that of the fig tree (Mk 13:28–29; Mt 24:32–33; Lk 21:29–31), has its antecedent in the OT wisdom literature (Prov 6:6–11).

A parable such as that of the wicked tenants (Mk 12:1–12; Mt 21:33–43; Lk 20:9–19) also has its precedent in a prophetic book (Isa 5:1–7). The exemplary story, such as that of the good Samaritan (Lk 10:29–37), has its antecedent in one of the OT historical books (2 Sam 14:4–13).

Thus a simply survey of this kind shows that the ancestors of the NT *parabolai* are to be found in the OT. To be sure, the Synoptic *parabolai* resemble most closely the rabbinic $m^e š\bar{a}l\hat{i}m$; but both have their antecedents in the earlier Semitic literature. There is no need to go outside the Semitic tradition to the classical tradition to explain the origin of any speech in the Synoptics which is there called a *parabolē*. This is not to deny that there could have been a Greek influence on the Semitic writings—on the wisdom collections, for example. But the Synoptic speeches trace their lineage directly to the OT and Jewish literature, and if they are related to the Greek literature at all, it is only indirectly through these. The important implication of this is that the problem of mysteriousness in the parables must be solved otherwise than by attributing the aspect of comparison to the Greek and the aspect of mystery to the Israelite tradition.

A word remains to be said about the meaning of the term *māšāl/parabolē*. It is readily apparent from the above survey and from the Appendix to this study that the term could refer to a variety of speeches in antiquity. The meaning of the term was evidently in flux and undefined in both the Semitic and classical traditions. All that can be said is that the words *māšāl* and *parabolē* were used by the ancients to refer to any unusual or striking speech. Their meanings were no more precise than this.

In modern scholarship such terms should, however, be defined as sharply as possible. If the definition is more precise in contemporary scientific writings than in the ancient sources, that should create no difficulty; it means only that the words are used differently in antiquity and in the present, which in itself is not a problem. There is no reason not to use the modern terms *proverb* and *wisdom saying* for those two kinds of speech. The term *parable* (in the broad sense) should be reserved for those speeches which are narrative in form, that is, which tell a story; a more precise definition will be proposed in the section below on parable and allegory. The term *fable*, incidentally, is best limited to those narratives in which the characters are usually animals, plants, or inanimate objects, and which have a prudential lesson; and the term *parable* for those narratives in which the characters are human beings, which have a religious or moral lesson, and which apparently are typically Semitic.

B. THE PARABLE AS LITERATURE

It will be helpful to keep in mind as a general framework for all of the following remarks the three component parts of any speech act. These are (A) *the producer*, that is, the speaker or writer; (B) *the speech* itself; and (C) *the receiver*, that is, the hearer or reader. The field of data of literary studies includes these three. It is of course (B), the speech itself, which is the primary object of interest in literary studies, but since all speech is to some extent communicative, and therefore involves an interaction between minds, (A) and (C) also legitimately come under its purview.

When we speak of the *meaning* of a literary work (as those who discuss the parables frequently must), we are really speaking of three different aspects of meaning which are related to (A), (B), and (C) respectively. Meaning in the speech itself is *reference*; meaning in the mind of the producer is *intention*; and meaning in the mind of the receiver is *interpretation*. The first, reference, is on the verbal or extra-mental level, and is objective; the other two, intention and interpretation, are on the psychological or mental level, and are subjective. The term "meaning" is somewhat broad, and is therefore less useful in literary discourse than these three distinct and precise senses of the word. Again, it is reference, the objective meaning in the speech itself, which is central, but what the speaker intends by the reference, and how the hearer interprets the reference, are facets of meaning which are far from negligible.

The speech itself is a structure which, like any other structure, consists of certain materials arranged in a certain form.[4] The materials out of which every speech is constructed are the elements of language, which is to say, sound and meaning, or sound which is meaningful. The materials are always the same; but the structures made of them can vary, for the elements of language can be organized according to different principles. The principle of organization is always supplied by what the speaker intends to be the purpose of the speech.

We may distinguish four such principles for the organization of language. One of these is *grammar*; it is grammatical or linguistic organization that gives meaning to a speech and so enables it to achieve the goal of effective communication. Another is *logic*; logical organization orders language toward the goal of communicating meaning that is specifically logical. Another is *rhetoric*, which is the artistic arrangement of language in such a way that it will achieve the goal of persuasiveness, of moving the addressee to decision or action.

In grammar, logic, and rhetoric, the principle of organization is external to the speech, being derived from its extrinsic or social purpose. It is

---

4. On speech, and its different kinds, see La Drière, "Rhetoric and 'Merely Verbal' Art"; "Structure, Sound, and Meaning"; and "Literary Form and Form in the Other Arts."

different with the other kind of structuring of language, which is the *aesthetic* or *poetic*. Here, the principle of organization seems to be internal, being derived from the sounds and meanings themselves. The poetic is the structuring of the intrinsic properties of the elements of language itself, of sounds and meanings. The producer simply creates patterns of sounds and patterns of meanings, which are there only to be contemplated by the receiver. The poetic, then, is structure of language for its own sake, without any goal beyond itself. Thus the aesthetic is coherence of structure as such. There is of course coherence in grammatical, logical, and rhetorical structures, otherwise they would not be structures at all; but it is only in the aesthetic that we have a concern for structure simply for itself.

Structures of all four of these kinds are present in any speech, and of any speech it is possible to do a grammatical, a logical, a rhetorical, and a poetical analysis, though in practice we usually analyze only those structures which are important and relevant. For not all of them are present in a speech to the same degree. What occurs in fact is that one organizing principle is dominant and the others more or less subordinate, so that there result speeches of four different kinds. Where the dominant organizing principle is grammar, we have everyday conversation or common prose; where it is logic, we have philosophic or scientific exposition (as in a scholarly essay); where it is rhetoric, we have propaganda or literary prose; and where it is the aesthetic, we have poetry. These are the traditional and still the most useful divisions of speech.

It was said above that the principle of organization of a speech is provided by the speaker's purpose. The goal of grammatical structure is satisfactory communication, which is a social process; the goal of logical structure is the conveyance of philosophic or scientific meaning, also a social process; the goal of rhetorical structure is persuasion, again a social process. The semantic or pragmatic purpose of these three kinds of speech lies outside the speech itself. Each is a structure, but a structure made to function as an instrument in a social process. With poetical structure it is not so. Here we have speech which has no purpose outside itself, which is to say that we have a structure which has no function. In a poem, which is, incidentally, a rare phenomenon, relations of sound and of meaning exist for their own sake, and not to serve any extrinsic or social goal.

The field of literature includes the last two kinds of speech, *rhetoric* and *poetic*. The term "literature" itself is not easy to define sharply, and for that reason it is less satisfactory than the terms rhetoric and poetic. Nevertheless, it is correct to say that the object of literary studies has traditionally been both the rhetorical, a practical or utilitarian art, and the poetical, a fine art.[5]

5. The two kinds of literature have their counterpart in the other arts, e.g., in the visual arts which include the fine art of painting and the practical or utilitarian art of architecture. See La Drière, "Literary Form and Form in the Other Arts," 37.

(The distinction between rhetoric and poetic is not, it should be noted, the same as that between prose and verse, for verse is often rhetorical, and prose may be poetic.) What literature studies in rhetoric is primarily its communicative property. It examines the construct in terms of its function, analyzing structures of sounds and meanings as instruments which contribute to achieving an effect in the hearer. What literature studies in the poetic is primarily structuredness itself. It examines the construct in terms of its intrinsic character, analyzing structures of sounds and meanings as such. If we recall our framework of (A) the producer, (B) the speech, and (C) the receiver, we shall readily see that in poetic the emphasis is on (B), the verbal construct, whereas in rhetoric it is on (C), the receiver.

It should by now be clear that the adjective "autonomous" cannot be applied to all literature indiscriminately. It might be pointed out that the term "autonomous," which means "making or having one's own laws,"[6] is not in any case the best word to use here. A more accurate term is "autotelic: having an end or purpose in and not apart from itself." It is correct to attribute to literary critics the view that art is autotelic, an end rather than a means; but, as has been seen, this is true only of the fine arts, such as poetic, not of the practical arts, such as rhetoric, which are "heterotelic: existing for the sake of something else; having an extraneous end or purpose."[7] Thus the problem of whether or not literary works are autotelic is easily resolved once the distinction between rhetoric and poetic is seen. It must be said that certain works of literary theory themselves fail to make this most important of distinctions.

It is not difficult to find the place of the Bible in this scheme of things. The biblical writings are essentially rhetorical; that is true of the Bible as a whole, of most of the books within the Bible, and of most of the smaller units within the books, including those most striking speeches of Jesus, the parables. A few of the writings—for example, the Song of Songs and some of the psalms—are, of course, poetic. But even these, from the viewpoint of larger purpose, function rhetorically, since their incorporation into a series (the Bible) is heterotelic. It is the rhetorical character of the biblical writings which some NT scholars have discerned and described so well in pointing out to us that the Gospels are not primarily biography or history but *kerygma*, or that the parables are "language-events." The parables are literature, to be sure, but they are certainly not poetry, for it never happens that the aesthetic structures in them gain the ascendancy; when they occur, as they do, it is only that they might contribute to the parables' rhetorical aim. It has often been remarked that it is because the parables are aesthetic that they have the power to move the hearer to decision or action. In reply to this, it must be said that if the poetic structures in the parables became dominant, their power to achieve an effect in the hearer would then be lost.

---

6. *The Oxford English Dictionary*, s.v. "autonomous."
7. *Webster's Third New International Dictionary*, s.v. "autotelic" and "heterotelic."

The parables, then, are by no means independent of a social context, or autotelic.

C. PARABLE AND ALLEGORY

The question of the relation between parable and allegory is separate from that of the parable's rhetorical and instrumental character. The two problems should be kept apart, and not pulled together as they frequently are.

It will be useful, at the outset, to define some of the most important terms employed in the classification of literary works.[8] One of these is *form*, a classification founded on structure of meaning. There are three basic literary forms. The first is called (1) expository or discursive, a form based on static reference to idea (e.g., exposition, essay) or thing (e.g., description). The other two may be called narratory, a term which includes any work that tells a story; they are (2) narrative (e.g., novel, short story), and (3) dramatic (e.g., play, dialogue). These are forms based on dynamic reference to event. Differences of voice and address are also involved in the classification of forms (as in the distinction between novel and play).

Another term is *genre*, a classification based on the nature, and not on the structure, of meaning. The genre of a work is determined by the object to which it refers—for example, heroes in epic, shepherds in pastoral, the marvelous in romance; or by the subjective mood or attitude toward the object, as in satire and comedy; or by both, as in tragedy, where the object referred to and the mood are equally serious. There are as many genres as there are subjects about which one can speak or write, and attitudes one may have toward them.

Another classification, important for the purposes of this study, is *mode of meaning*, also a structural distinction. There are only two modes of meaning: direct or literal meaning; and indirect or tropical meaning (usually but inaccurately called figurative), an example of which is allegory.

It is helpful to keep all of these types of classification separate, and to know that when we speak of a literary work such as Spenser's *Faerie Queene*, we are speaking of a composition the form of which is narrative, the genre romance, and the mode of meaning allegorical. Thus it is possible for a literary composition to share with the *Faerie Queene* the allegorical mode of meaning while differing greatly from it in other respects. These distinctions in classification can contribute much toward unraveling the problem of parable and allegory and their relation to each other.

Perhaps the best starting-point for a discussion of parable and allegory is with two devices of speech known as the figure and the trope.[9] A figure consists only of some striking arrangement—or figuration—of language; it

---

8. See La Drière, "Classification, Literary."

9. Figures and tropes are treated in the handbooks and dictionaries of literature cited in note 1 of this chapter.

involves no change in meaning, since all the words are used literally. In a trope, on the other hand, the meaning of the words is indeed changed. Following are examples of both literary devices.

One example of a *figure* is the simile. A simile is a comparison, employing the word "like" or "as," of two things, but only of two things which are more unlike than alike. It is a simile to say "Achilles rushed on like a lion," but not to say, "Achilles rushed on like a brave soldier." Similes occur occasionally in the NT, as in the sayings, "be wise as serpents and innocent as doves" (Mt 10:16), and "you are like white-washed tombs" (Mt 23:27).

Another figure is periphrasis or circumlocution, which consists in saying in many words what could be said in a few, or roundabout what could be said straightforwardly. It is circumlocution, for example, to say that someone "has gone to his rest." We have an instance of periphrasis in the wisdom saying, "there is nothing outside a man which by going into him can defile him; / but the things which come out of a man are what defile him" (Mk 7:15; Mt 15:11). The expression, "nothing outside a man which by going into him" is circumlocution for food; and the expression "the things which come out of a man" is circumlocution for his thoughts, words, and deeds.

Since the *trope*, or *tropical meaning*, plays an essential part in both allegory and parable, it will now be explained in some detail. All meaning, as has been said, may be divided into two modes; these are popularly referred to as literal and figurative, but are more accurately called direct and indirect, or primary and secondary, or literal and tropical. The trope is a device of speech which is discussed at great length in ancient works of rhetoric and which continues to be one of the subjects of most interest in modern literary studies. A good definition is that of Quintilian: "By a *trope* is meant the artistic alteration of a word or phrase from its proper meaning to another" (*Institutio* VIII.vi.1). A trope, as its name implies, is a turn or change which occurs when an unexpected word is placed in a syntactic structure and is thereby given another meaning in addition to its literal one. Thus a trope is a syntactic modification of the lexical. *In every trope, then, the word has two levels of meaning, the direct or literal, and the indirect or tropical.* Between the two levels of meaning there is both similarity and dissimilarity, with sometimes the one predominating, sometimes the other. There are numerous kinds of tropes, or subtle shifts in meaning; indeed, the list is endless. It will suffice to define only a few of them here.

The most common trope is the metaphor. A metaphor is the substitution of the name of one thing for the name of another, so that one or more properties of the first are attributed to the second. We have seen Aristotle's example, "The lion rushed forward," where "lion" is substituted for "Achilles," and certain qualities associated with the lion are thus attributed to him. In this metaphor we have a good illustration of the two levels of meaning present in every trope. The word "lion" makes a direct reference to a certain species of animal; but the animal in turn suggests such attributes as strength and courage, and so there is an indirect reference to a man who displays these qualities. In a metaphor, the word points to a thing (lion), and that thing in turn points to another thing (Achilles). The metaphor also illustrates the similarity and dissimilarity present in every trope. Like the simile, a metaphor always has to do with two things which are in one or a few respects alike, but are for the most part quite unlike; this is true for example of Achilles and a lion. Metaphors occur quite frequently in the Gospels, for example in the sayings, "go rather to the lost sheep of the house of Israel" (Mt 10:6) and "You brood of vipers¹" (Mt 12:34).

It should be said, against the curious slandering of the metaphor in much NT scholarship, that this trope has always been held in high regard by literary theorists. Aristotle wrote that of the various devices of speech, "by far the greatest thing is the use of metaphor. That alone cannot be learned; it is the token of genius. For the right use of metaphor means a perception of the similarity in dissimilar things" (*Poetics* XXII.16–17).[10] Quintilian called the metaphor "the commonest and by far the most beautiful of tropes," adding:

> It is not merely so natural a turn of speech that it is often employed unconsciously or by uneducated persons, but it is in itself so attractive and elegant that however distinguished the language in which it is embedded it shines forth with a light that is all its own.
>
> (*Institutio* VIII.vi.4)

Synecdoche, another kind of trope, is also the substitution of the name of one thing for the name of another, in this case of the part for the whole, the singular for the plural, the individual for the species, the species for the genus—or the reverse of all these. We employ synecdoche when we say "hands" to mean workmen, "sails" to mean ships, and "our daily bread" to mean our daily sustenance. In synecdoche there is more similarity than dissimilarity between the two things compared.

Still another trope is metonymy, the substition of the name of one thing for the name of another thing with which it is closely associated: the inventor for the invention, the author for his works, the container for the thing contained, the effect for the cause, and so on. Thus we say "Shakespeare" for Shakespeare's works, and "the crown" for the king. In Genesis we read, "In the sweat of your face you shall eat bread" (3:19), where "sweat" means hard labor; and in the Gospels we read of "a house divided against itself" (Mk 3:25; Mt 12:25; Lk 11:17), where "house" means family or dynasty.

Irony is a trope in which the literal meaning of the words is contrary to the speaker's intention. The intention is usually conveyed by such means as the speaker's tone of voice, or the context of the remark. Most often irony uses words of praise or approval to imply blame or disapproval, but the opposite

---

10. Aristotle *Poetics* (tr. W. Hamilton Fyfe; rev. ed.; *LCL*; Cambridge: Harvard University Press, 1932). Some changes have here been made in the translation by Fyfe.

can also occur. In irony, the element of dissimilarity is far greater than the element of similarity, since the literal and tropical meanings are opposites. There is irony in Mark Antony's oration over the dead Caesar, when he insists that "Brutus is an honourable man" (Shakespeare *Julius Caesar* III.ii). A striking example from the Bible is Job's remark to his counselors: "No doubt you are the people, and wisdom will die with you" (Job 12:2).

The trope, strictly speaking, is a device of speech involving a modification in one or a few words, in small units of meaning or micro-meanings. But such change can occur also in large units of meaning, in macro-meanings or whole compositions. We have an example of irony extended over a whole work, to cite but one trope, in Jonathan Swift's *A Modest Proposal*, ostensibly a political pamphlet suggesting that the Irish sell their infants to the English landlords to save a starving Ireland. When a double meaning is present across an entire work, we may say, by analogy, that the whole work is tropical. What is most important to note is that this effect is *sometimes* achieved by the use of tropes in individual words, but not always, for *the whole meaning can be tropical even when the constituent meanings are not.*

We are now prepared to formulate an accurate definition of allegory. Perhaps no single thing would contribute more toward disposing of the difficulties that still hamper our understanding of the parables. An *allegory* is the extension over a whole story of the most common and beautiful of the tropes, the metaphor. It is nothing more and nothing less than *an extended metaphor in narratory form* (the term narratory here being used to include both dramatic and narrative works, that is, all works which tell a story).[11] An allegory, then, is quite simply a story in which there are two levels of meaning, the literal and the metaphorical. Our definition says *extended* metaphor, not series of metaphors; again the distinction between constituent meanings and the whole meaning must be stressed. It cannot be overemphasized that there is no need for the metaphorical use of single words in the presentation of an allegory. The author may, of course, use metaphors on the way to creating an allegorical story, but he does not have to. What occurs in the metaphor simply occurs in the allegory over a broader range. Despite repeated assertions to the contrary during decades of scholarship on the parables, therefore, it is not the presence or absence of metaphors in the constituent meanings which determines whether or not a story is an allegory, but only the presence or absence of metaphor in the whole meaning.

Allegory, then, is simply a device of meaning, and not in itself a literary form or genre. Rather, it appears in literary works of many kinds. It can be put to either rhetorical or poetical uses, and it can occur, as has been said, in any narratory work, whether long or short, in verse or in prose. There are allegorical novels (Golding's *Lord of the Flies*), short stories (Hawthorne's "Young Goodman Brown"), and plays (*Everyman*), to name but a few

11. See the definition of allegory in Holman, *A Handbook to Literature.*

possibilities—and, what is of most interest to us, there are allegorical fables and parables.[12]

Any parable which has both a literal and a metaphorical meaning is an allegory. The *discrimen* of the parable, what distinguishes it from other allegories, is its rhetorical purpose, more specifically, its particular religious or ethical rhetorical purpose. Thus we have an allegory, for example, in the parable of the prodigal son (Lk 15:11–32), on one level the story of a lost son's return home to his father, on another level a lesson about God's merciful love toward repentant sinners. We have an allegory in the parable of the importunate friend (Lk 11:5–10), on one level the story of a man imploring his reluctant friend for three loaves of bread at a most inconvenient time, the middle of the night, on another level a precept on persistence in prayer. We have an allegory in the parable of the unmerciful servant (Mt 18:21–25), on one level the story of a man whose master had released him of his heavy debt out of pity, but who in turn refused to remit the debt of a fellow servant who owed him much less, on another level an exhortation to forgive others as God forgives us. These parables, and many others, are quite alike in having a metaphorical effect in the whole meaning, and no distinction is to be made among them on the basis of whether or not there are metaphors in the individual words.

There are, of course, other tropes and figures besides the metaphor at work in the parables. A number of parables are based on the simile. These include all those which begin with the formula "The kingdom of God is like"—e.g., the weeds among the wheat (Mt 13:24–30,36–43), the marriage feast (Mt 22:1–14; Lk 14:15–24), and the laborers in the vineyard (Mt 20:1–16). Jülicher, it will be recalled, said that all parables are based on the simile; while that is not true of all, it is certainly true of many.

It was said above that the simile is not a trope, but a figure. Nevertheless, the use of the simile can also result in a tropical meaning in the whole parable—and this is further evidence that we can have the tropical mode in the whole meaning even when the constituent meanings are non-tropical. If a simile is extended far enough, it develops into something which hardly differs from an extended metaphor or an allegory.[13] We may take as an example the parable of the weeds among the wheat (Mt 13:24–30). The brief introduction, "The kingdom of heaven may be compared to a man who sowed good seed," is a simile of sorts; but as the parable goes on, we begin to get two levels of meaning, and what we have in the entire parable is nothing other than a tropical narrative. On one level it tells the story of a man whose

12. Edwin Honig, in his monograph on allegory entitled *Dark Conceit: The Making of Allegory* (New York: Oxford University Press, 1959) 10, gives as an example of allegory Aesop's fable of the quarrel of the belly and the limbs quoted in Shakespeare's *Coriolanus* I.i.

13. The same point is made by Lanham in his article on "Trope" in *A Handlist of Rhetorical Terms*, 103. There he discusses a speech from *Euphues* which is constructed exclusively of figures, but which as a whole is metaphorical.

enemies sow weeds in his field of wheat, but who allows both to grow together until the harvest, when the weeds are separated and burned; on another level it teaches that God permits the good and the evil to co-exist until the end of time, when they are divided at the judgment. Both metaphor and simile, then, when extended over a whole narrative, result in allegory.

Allegory does not, however, exhaust the parables, for not all parables are allegories. There are some which Jülicher, correctly recognizing as different, set apart from the others and called exemplary stories; these are the good Samaritan (Lk 10:29–37), the rich fool (Lk 12:16–21), the rich man and Lazarus (Lk 16:19–31), and the Pharisee and the tax collector (Lk 18:9–14). What we have in these parables is something akin to synecdoche, the name of the part for the whole, or the one for the many. They are not extended metaphors; rather they present one particular example to illustrate a general principle, and so might be called extended synecdoches.

A current misconception is that exemplary story and parable are distinguished by this, that the exemplary story is strictly literal while the parable is tropical.[14] In fact, however, the exemplary story (an extended synecdoche) is as much a tropical composition as the parable (an extended metaphor or an allegory). This is because synecdoche and metaphor are equally tropes. No exemplary story is intended to be taken only literally. The good Samaritan, for example, is on the literal level a story about a Samaritan who aids a wounded man whom the Jewish priest and Levite had passed by, and on the tropical level a lesson of supreme importance, that the person who does the concrete deed of love for the neighbor, and not necessarily the official member of the established religion, is the one who carries out the requirements of God.

These are but a few examples; a close study of the parables would undoubtedly yield an abundance of both figures and tropes. Whatever the figure or trope which serves as its framework, however, *every parable has two levels of meaning; that is, every parable as a whole is tropical*. If the parables did not have a double meaning, they would have hardly any point at all. The double-meaning effect is a *sine qua non* of the parable.[15]

---

14. See, for example, John Dominic Crossan, "Parable and Example in the Teaching of Jesus," *NTS* 18 (1971–72) 285–307. (Reprinted in *Semeia* 1 [1974] 63–104.) There Crossan (especially pp. 285–86) adopts the view of Bultmann, *Synoptic Tradition* (pp. 177–78) that exemplary stories differ from other parables in that they alone are not "figurative" (i.e., tropical). Jülicher himself, however, as has been noted, held that *all* parables (similitudes, parables, and exemplary stories) are literal speech, and that it is precisely this which distinguishes them from allegory. (See above, Chapter I, Section A, especially note 8.)

15. To spell out further the concept of literal speech: To maintain that a parable is strictly literal would be to say, for example, that the prodigal son is only a narrative about *this* particular father and his two sons; or the weeds among the wheat simply a story about a farmer's difficulties with his crop; or the good Samaritan merely a tale about a wounded man who was at last given help by the third person to pass by. To grant that there is more meaning than this in the parables is to agree that they are tropical.

The *parable*, then, may be defined as follows: It is a structure consisting of *a tropical narrative, or a narrative having two levels of meaning*; this structure functions as *religious or ethical rhetorical speech*.

The definition proposed here includes Jülicher's similitude, parable, and exemplary story. The similitude is distinguished from the other two insofar as it narrates a typical occurrence in real life (rather than a fictitious event), as Jülicher said. The exemplary story is distinguished from the other two insofar as it is composed of extended synedoche (rather than allegory). All three are tropical narratives intended as rhetoric.

It would of course be possible to argue that this definition applies only to the parables as they appear in the Gospels, that is, that Jesus himself spoke exclusively in parables that were extended similes, and not in the other kinds of parables described here. But that is hardly defensible in view of the fact that the OT and rabbinic $m^e\check{s}al\bar{\imath}m$ are also based on figures and tropes of various kinds.

All of this is not to say that the interpretations appended to the parables in the Synoptic Gospels are all original. Doubtless some of them are secondary, produced by the Church or the evangelist. An interpretation can be recognized as secondary, however, not because it is "allegorical"—but because it differs in two or three Gospels, or because it does not fit the parable itself, or because it reflects the situation of the primitive Church. The original meaning of a parable is just as tropical as a secondary interpretation.

It should by now be clear to what extent the way in which allegory and parable are usually contrasted is misconceived. In the first place, the definition of parable as an extended simile is inadequate, since a parable can be an extension of metaphor, simile, synecdoche, or some other trope or figure. Moreover, the definition of allegory as a sequence of metaphors is inaccurate; it is rather an *extended* metaphor. This means that allegory and parable are certainly not differentiated on the basis of whether there is one point of comparison or many. This fallacious distinction has misled scholars into dividing parables into three groups, "pure parable," "pure allegory," and "mixed type"—depending on how many metaphors can be discerned in them; in fact, most of the narratives usually so classified are both allegory and parable, or rather, allegorical parables. Finally, to maintain that the parable is literal speech, the allegory figurative—by which is meant tropical—speech, is likewise incorrect; both parable and allegory have two levels of meaning, the literal and tropical.

Neither is it correct to say that a parable is aesthetic while an allegory is not. If anything is true, it is the opposite. As has been said, a parable is never an aesthetic or poetic construct. On the other hand, an allegory can be, though it does not have to be, since allegory can serve either poetical or rhetorical purposes. It seems self-evident that an allegory like Spenser's *Faerie Queene* is far more aesthetic than any parable in the Gospels.

To say of a literary object, "This is not allegory; it is a parable," is, in sum, an error in *logic*. Allegory (not by itself a literary form or genre) is only a component of some parables. Thus there are allegorical stories that are not parables, and parables that are not allegorical. The error—which has so clouded the study of parables—results from a fundamental confusion of categories. (See the beginning of this section, on the classification of literary works.)

At this point the parable may be considered in relation to the notion of "mystery." The discussion that follows here is concerned with only one aspect of "mystery," namely, that implicit in parabolic speech; a fuller discussion of the concept of mystery in the Semitic tradition and in the Gospel of Mark is set forth in Chapter 4.

It will be recalled that, as Lagrange, T. W. Manson, and Hermaniuk pointed out, the OT and Jewish literature frequently speak of the $m^e\check{s}\bar{a}l\bar{\imath}m$ as mysterious (see above, Chapter 1, Section B, especially note 13). In particular, we have three instances where the hearer utterly fails to grasp the point of the parable (2 Sam 12:1–14; 14:4–13; 1 Kgs 20:39–42). In addition, there is the theory of the mysteriousness of parables expressed in the Gospel of Mark, most explicitly in chapter 4. It is now possible to address the crucial question to which much of the research on parables is directed: *why is it that the parables were understood as mysterious in this ancient Jewish and Christian literature?* The answer is that it is precisely because they employ the tropical mode of meaning. The structure of double meaning present in every parable makes possible its functioning as mysterious speech. This effect is achieved when the parable is placed in a social situation, that is, when it is made a means of interaction between two persons, the speaker and the hearer. It requires, that is, the three component parts of a speech act. (A) The speaker pronounces the parable; (B) the parable itself has two levels of meaning; (C) the hearer may or may not apprehend its indirect and more important level of meaning—thus it is "mysterious." The mysteriousness, then, consists quite simply in the hearer's inability or unwillingness to comprehend the indirect or tropical meaning of the parable. Or, one could say that the mysteriousness comprises the two levels of meaning *plus* the hearer's failure to grasp the second level.

The fact that they are tropical does not necessarily mean that all parables are difficult to comprehend—for obviously many are not—but it does make possible the rise of a tradition about their mysterious character. It is not *necessary* that they be understood as mysterious; it is *possible*. There is no predetermination in this; one culture may regard them as quite clear, another as somewhat obscure. That the Greek and Latin literatures never exploited this aspect of fables and parables in the way that the Semitic literature did is an accident of history. It does not stem from any significant difference in the fables and parables produced by the two cultures. The Greeks and Romans, who engaged in literary theory, recognized the presence of two levels of meaning in some words and whole compositions, and used such scientific terms as "trope" and "allegory" to speak of this; but they did not pay much attention to the fact that the hearer can sometimes fail to grasp the tropical meaning, and so never developed the notion of mysteriousness. The Israelites of course did not engage in literary theory; they realized nevertheless that it is possible for the hearer to miss the real meaning of the mā́šāl, and used the quasi-religious term "mystery" to speak of this. Whatever their manner of viewing it, the literary phenomenon in question—the tropical composition—is the same in the two cultures.

We know from the many references in the biblical and related literature that the tradition regarding the mā́šāl or parable as mysterious existed from at least the time of writing of the books of Samuel and Kings down to the NT period. We can observe interesting variations in the tradition as we trace its history down through the centuries. Three parables in the historical books, Nathan's ewe lamb (2 Sam 12:1–14), the wise woman of Tekoa's two brothers and the avengers (2 Sam 14:4–13), and the anonymous prophet's escaped prisoner (1 Kgs 20:39–42), are employed as devices to trick the hearer into pronouncing judgment on himself; they depend for their success on the use of indirect reference. The idea expressed in the wisdom books (Prov 1:5b–6; Sir 39:2–3; 47:15 in the LXX; 47:17 in the Hebrew) that parables are enigmatic and require learned interpretation is no doubt connected with the increasing sophistication in composing and commenting on proverbs and parables in the schools of the scribes. Occasionally in the prophetic books parables are the medium of obscure oracular speech (Ezek 17:2; Hab 2:6). In apocalyptic works (1 Enoch 68:1) they become the vehicle of revelation of heavenly and eschatological secrets. Still another variation on the theme of mysteriousness appears in the Gospel of Mark; the special Markan use of the parables will be the subject of Chapters 4 and 5 of this study.

All of this is not to say that every parable is intended to obscure. A parable is an implied comparison. Since it is only implied, there must be some insight on the part of the hearer if it is to be apprehended. The comparison is not always obvious; but once it is grasped by the hearer it sheds fresh light on the subject under discussion. The purpose of a parable is ultimately to instruct, or more accurately to move to decision or action; but this is done through indirect rather than direct reference.

3

PROBLEMS IN THE STUDY OF PARABLES

Anyone who has dealt with the Synoptic parables cannot but be aware of the many problems involved in their study. The exegete must undertake such difficult tasks as arriving at accurate interpretations of the parables, determining whether Jesus could have uttered "complex" as well as "simple" parables, and deciding whether individual parables and their Synoptic explanations are authentic. The remarks presented here have as their aim, not to resolve the problems surrounding any single parable, but to provide the theoretical framework within which these essential tasks can best be carried out.

A. THE PROBLEM OF INTERPRETATION

The parables have been given so many different interpretations over the last two millennia that the question of how correctly to construe their meaning naturally arises. The problem of interpretation is, again, an effect of the parables' tropical character, for it is really the problem of establishing the second level of meaning. There are few difficulties in determining the first or literal meaning, but what that in turn suggests is not always immediately evident, or is not always fixed; hence the process of interpretation may fairly be called problematic.

The problem of interpretation can best be worked out within the general scheme for the component parts of a speech act which was set down at the outset. It will be recalled that the three specific senses of the term "meaning" are (A) *intention*, meaning in the mind of the speaker, which is psychological or subjective; (B) *reference*, meaning in the speech, which is verbal or objective; and (C) *interpretation*, meaning in the mind of the hearer, which is also psychological or subjective. The meaning of a trope involves all three of these, and not just (B), the reference.

Apprehending the meaning of any trope requires perceiving what the speaker intends. This is most evident, perhaps, in irony. When Job says, "No doubt you are the people, and wisdom will die with you" (Job 12:2), and means quite the contrary, the meaning is much more in his intention than in the reference of the words. A correct interpretation of the meaning therefore requires a correct interpretation of the speaker's intention. Indeed, without intention and interpretation there is no trope here at all, for there is nothing whatsoever in the words alone, or the reference, to point to a different meaning. Since what produces the trope of irony is that the intention and reference are opposite, the hearer must interpret both in order to grasp the whole ironic meaning. This example illustrates how much subjectivity is at work in all tropical meaning.

Apprehending the meaning of a trope also requires perceiving, or interpreting, the natural as well as the conventional meaning of the words. By conventional meaning is meant the dictionary definition of a word, what is sometimes called its denotation; this is the meaning agreed upon by all who speak a common language. By natural meaning is meant the associations awakened by a word, what is sometimes called its connotation. To use Aristotle's example once again, that the word "lion" refers to a certain species of animal is conventional meaning; but that the lion suggests the attributes of prowess and might is natural meaning. In some cases natural meaning is communal, that is, peculiar to a certain region or culture. For example, bread and wine suggest life-giving sustenance only in some countries; in others, it would be different food and drink. Black is the color suggesting mourning in some traditions, white in others. In such instances, only the person acquainted with the tradition will grasp the natural meaning.

A little reflection will bring out the natural meaning in the images in the parables. For example, the sowing of seed quite naturally suggests the dissemination of a thing; wheat and weeds suggest good and evil things respectively; imprisonment suggests punishment in general; a feast suggests rejoicing. Caution is always necessary in the matter of natural meaning, however. Natural meaning is only *suggested* meaning, and it requires a measure of perceptivity on the part of the hearer if it is to be apprehended at all. Moreover, natural meaning is never as clear and definite as conventional meaning, and in specific cases it is often subject to debate.

Tropical meaning, then, involves a crossing of the objective and the subjective, and a crossing of the conventional and the natural. It is this that makes it both uncommonly striking and effective speech, and speech that is by no means simple and straightforward to interpret.

Surely the first circle of hearers, those who heard the parables from the lips of Jesus, asked "What does the man mean?" They must have wondered, that is, about his intention. This was conveyed to them no doubt in various ways. Perhaps the discussion or question which preceded a parable gave the clue to its meaning. Perhaps Jesus sometimes gave an explicit interpretation following the parable, as the rabbinic literature portrays the rabbis as doing. Certainly Jesus and his Jewish audience shared a common stock of metaphors. As is well known, in the rabbinic parables God was often represented as a king, a judge, a father, the owner of a vineyard or field; the people Israel were depicted as his servants, his sons, his vine or flock; the judgment was represented as a harvest or a reckoning; and the kingdom as a feast or a wedding. The (sometimes communal) natural meaning in these metaphors would not have been lost on the audience. Thus, from one or all of these clues, they would have been able to interpret the intention of Jesus.

Those of us who hear or read the parables centuries later must proceed to an interpretation of Jesus' intention in much the same way. The natural meaning in the parables is often fairly evident, at least to those familiar with the Christian tradition. Further clues to Jesus' intention are provided by a knowledge of his eschatological and ethical teaching, and by a knowledge of first-century Palestinian Judaism. The fact that the task of establishing the original meaning of the parables is a difficult one, and that in some cases it is not possible to arrive at certainty, does not justify abandoning it altogether. The historical studies of the parables by Dodd, Jeremias, and others are legitimate and in some (if not all) instances quite illuminating.

It should now be clear that the original meaning of a parable and a later interpretation are equally tropical. A secondary interpretation changes the indirect level of meaning; it does not add it, for a double meaning is inherent in the parable as a literary construct. As an example, we may take the parable of the sower and its interpretation (Mk 4:1–9,13–20). The Markan explanation does not distort the nature of the narrative; it does not transform one kind of speech (a parable) into another kind of speech (an allegory). The parable itself is an allegory—whether its original indirect level of meaning be that the kingdom will come despite all obstacles; or that the labor of the disciples will in the end be successful despite initial failures; or that the hearer must receive and keep the word proclaimed by Jesus (or the Christian preacher) in the face of all temptations.[1] Each of these explanations takes the parable, rightly, as an allegory. No one interpretation may be rejected on the grounds that it is more allegorical than another. To be sure, the question of the original meaning of the parable must be addressed by the exegete; but its answer does not at all depend on an allegory/parable dichotomy.

It may be added that even those modern interpretations of the parables that purport to move away altogether from the allegorical are in fact tropical. The parable of the prodigal son (Lk 15:11–32) is a case in point. Some reject the traditional view that the story is a lesson about the relation of man to God because this interpretation takes the parable as an extended metaphor, or an allegory. To say, however, that it is a lesson only about the relation of man to man—a lesson on human love—is still to assign to it a tropical meaning, for this interpretation takes the parable as an extended synecdoche, or to use Jülicher's term, an exemplary story.[2] Neither explanation understands the narrative absolutely literally, that is, as a story only

1. These are some of the possible meanings of the parable of the sower suggested by D. E. Nineham, *The Gospel of St Mark*, The Pelican New Testament Commentaries (Baltimore: Penguin Books, 1963) 135. The parable is discussed further in Chapter 4 of this study.

2. Jeremias, *Parables*, adopts the view that the parable of the prodigal son has to do with repentant sinners and God's mercy toward them (pp. 128–32). Via, *Parables*, appears to hold that it has to do only with human interrelationships (p. 106), though in his exegesis of the parable (pp. 162–76) he admits, secondarily, the religious interpretation.

about this particular father and his two sons; both see in it further meaning. All that has been done in the second interpretation is that the tropical meaning has been changed from extended metaphor to extended synecdoche. The basic question is which of these meanings was intended by Jesus when he uttered the parable. Both the preaching of Jesus in general, and the natural meaning in the characters of the younger brother, the elder brother, and the father, as well as in the story as a whole, would seem to indicate that the intention of Jesus was to teach about God's mercy.

A view sometimes expressed in recent literature on parables is that the interpretations found in the Synoptics in some way distort or misrepresent the parables themselves—and that all of them may well be secondary. It is thought that the interpretations effect a shift from one type of speech, a challenging and transforming word-event, to another type of speech, something like "theologizing" or "allegorizing," which is less faithful to the subject and the method of Jesus' teaching.[3] The question must be addressed whether such a transmutation does occur in the process of interpretation. It should be made clear, therefore, how a parable and its interpretation are related, and how they are alike and how they differ as speech constructs.

A parable, like any tropical narrative, is *a narrative to discursive effect*. The *narrative*, or the story itself (e.g., the unmerciful servant), is the direct, literal meaning of a parable; its *discursive effect*, or its lesson (e.g., the injunction to forgiveness), is the indirect, tropical meaning. As has been said, the discursive effect or lesson is not explicit in the words of the parable itself—not on the extra-mental or objective plane—but only implicit; it must be interpreted by the hearer—on the mental or subjective plane. A spoken or written interpretation simply attempts to state in explicit and literal terms what is implicit and tropical in the parable. The interpretation puts into words what is in the mind of the hearer. It expresses the lesson in direct and literal language. Such speech cannot be called in any sense a misrepresentation or a distortion—not, at least, if it is correct, that is, grounded in text and context. It is an altogether legitimate expression of meaning. This is true notwithstanding the fact that parable and interpretation differ in basic ways as literary constructs.

One of the main differences between a parable and its interpretation is the difference as to *mode of meaning*. It will be recalled that all speeches fall under only two modes, the direct or literal, and the indirect or tropical. The parable itself, of course, is tropical speech (having two levels of meaning), while its interpretation is literal speech (having one level of meaning only).

Another major difference between a parable and its interpretation is the difference as to *form*. The three basic literary forms, as said earlier, are expository or discursive, narrative, and dramatic speech. The parable is narrative (or dynamic reference to event); its interpretation is discourse (or

3. Such a line of argument seems to be the thrust of Part 1 of Via, *Parables*, for example.

static reference to idea). More specifically, the interpretation of a parable is always ethical or theological discourse.

If the parable and its interpretation differ as to mode of meaning and form, however, they do not differ as to *kind*. The four kinds of speech, as pointed out above, are ordinary, scientific, rhetorical, and poetic speech. These are distinctions based on the principle of organization of a speech, which principle is derived from its purpose. The parable and its interpretation are clearly alike in this respect, since both have as their primary purpose to persuade, convince, or move to decision or action. To effect a change in the hearer is as much the aim of the interpretation as it is of the parable.

A parable and its interpretation, then, differ as literary structures: a parable is a tropical narrative, while its interpretation is literal discourse. Both, however, function as rhetorical speech.

In that continual quest to find *the* difference between allegory and parable, the assertion has recently been made that in the case of an allegory the tropical meaning (or lesson) can be stated in expository prose and the literal meaning (or story) discarded without loss, whereas this cannot be done in the case of a parable.[4] This assertion simply cannot be demonstrated to be true. As has been said, all that the interpretation of *any* tropical narratory work does is to leave aside for the moment the literal meaning (or story) and to state the tropical meaning (or lesson) in expository prose. The indirect or tropical meaning of a parable not only can be, but often is, very well rendered in expository prose, in the Synoptics, in sermons, and in scholarly exegeses. Of course, in the case of *any* tropical story which is rhetorical, when this is done the rhetorical impact of the story itself is lost to some extent. A parable, being filled with imagery and action, and suggesting as it does that there is more meaning to be discovered here, has great power to catch and hold the attention of the hearer, and to be remembered long after it is heard. That is why it is able to teach its lesson more effectively than straightforward moral or theological discourse of the kind given in an interpretation. The interpretation, standing alone, does not arouse curiosity or strike the imagination as does the story. But the loss is in rhetorical effect, not in meaning (except insofar as the literal level of meaning is for the time being ignored). There is no difference whatsoever in this respect between a parable and any other rhetorical composition having two levels of meaning. To demonstrate this, one need only carry out the exercise of expressing the tropical meaning of any work generally agreed to be an allegory—say *Everyman* or *Pilgrim's Progress*—and of any parable in the Synoptic Gospels. The process of interpretation and the result will in every case be the same.

The conclusion to which these considerations from literary theory lead is

---

4. See Crossan, "Parable and Example," 304–306; and Norman Perrin, "Wisdom and Apocalyptic in the Message of Jesus," *SBL 1972 Proceedings*, Vol. II, 558, 566–67.

that, despite wide opinion to the contrary, there is nothing at all incongruous about the interpretations of the parables found in the Synoptic Gospels. Again, they certainly do not transform a parable into an allegory. They merely render the meaning or point of the parable in explicit and literal terms, which is a perfectly sensible enterprise.

This conclusion is corroborated by other considerations from the history of the Semitic and classical literatures. The explanations appended to the Synoptic parables are far from being unique in the ancient world. It is well known that parables and fables in the Old Testament and the rabbinic literature, as well as in the classical literature, are often accompanied by explanations. (This is true also of tropical compositions in the literature of many other cultures.) Were the Synoptic interpretations censured as inappropriate, the censure would have to cover similar interpretations in the entire traditions of Semitic and classical literature. Few, it is to be hoped, would wish to make such a blanket condemnation. Whether this *literary* tradition represents *historical* reality is another question. We cannot know with certainty how the parables and fables were employed in real life by the prophets, wise men, and rabbis in Israel, or the rhetoricians and politicians in Greece. But it is reasonable to suppose that the speakers themselves sometimes presented the explanations to their audience, since that is what the literature so often tells us. There is, moreover, nothing to suggest that Jesus would have employed the parables in a way different from that of any other rabbi.

Then, it cannot but be acknowledged that there is nothing objectionable about the presence of interpretations in the Synoptics, generally speaking. To say this is not to assert, however, that every interpretation—or for that matter every parable—goes back to the historical Jesus. As has been well established, that some are creations or modifications by the Church is highly probable. One task of the exegete is to assess the historicity of the parables and their explanations; but each case must be assessed individually.

It is a reality of history that the parables have been given many different interpretations from the beginning of the Synoptic tradition down to the present. A parable is not always interpreted in strict conformity with the original meaning. This fact raises the important but difficult question whether secondary interpretations are or are not permissible. Again, there are those who would argue, with Dodd and Jeremias, that an interpretation in line with the intention of Jesus is alone admissible; and there are those who would point out, with Via, that such a strictly "historical" approach may render the parables incapable of speaking to the present.

It may be helpful in this regard to distinguish between what is correct or incorrect, and what is valid or invalid. An example from the field of art may illustrate the distinction. A painting of the washing of the disciples' feet which depicted, or interpreted, all the figures as Chinese would be historically incorrect, of course, but few would regard it as artistically invalid. We frequently accept such incorrect works as valid. As for the parables, only an interpretation that stays within the limits of the intention of the speaker can be said to be correct. Yet tropical language is exceedingly rich; the reference can suggest special natural meanings to an individual hearer, so that he gives to the words his own interpretation which differs from the speaker's intention. A mind as profound and urbane as Augustine's, for example, would find in the parables a wealth of theological meaning. To say with Augustine that in the parable of the good Samaritan (Lk 10:29–37) the man who went down from Jerusalem to Jericho stands for Adam, the priest and Levite for the OT priesthood, and the Samaritan for the Lord, is probably not to follow the intention of Jesus, and this explanation is very likely incorrect.[5] Nevertheless, it cannot so readily be concluded that such an interpretation is invalid.

The question whether secondary interpretations are legitimate is, in part, a rhetorical one. The nuance of meaning of an interpretation is related to the *purpose* of the interpreter, and to the *use* or function of the interpretation. These are the determinants, not of the correctness of an interpretation, but of its character. The interpretation is shaped to a great extent by the larger context of ideas which the interpreter wishes to convey, and by his perception of the situation and needs of those to whom it is addressed. As these vary greatly in the history of Christianity, so do the interpretations of the parables. Such modifications, if well done, may be of considerable value rhetorically. An important safeguard is that the community of NT exegetes, and the individual interpreter, be aware of the distinction in general between the intention of the speaker, Jesus, and the interpretation of a theologian or preacher which adjusts a parable's meaning to a different time and place.

It is at this point that the work of the literary theorist ends, and that of the theologian begins. Only by theological debate can the issue be resolved whether secondary interpretations have a place in the history of Christian thought. Some would maintain, on theological as well as rhetorical grounds, that both tasks are legitimate and worthwhile: to attempt to recover the meanings of the parables as uttered by Jesus, and to adapt the parables to new situations in the Church.[6] The contribution which the literary theorist can make to the debate is to provide the clearest possible description of the parable as a literary construct, as a solid foundation on which to build.

B. "SIMPLE" AND "COMPLEX" PARABLES

A critical question raised by Jülicher remains to be addressed: did the historical Jesus employ "complex" parables, such as the sower as it is

---

5. Augustine, *Quaestiones Evangeliorum*, II.19; quoted by Dodd, *Parables*, 1–2.
6. The emergence of redaction criticism will perhaps lead to more sympathetic attention to Synoptic interpretations of the parables, and to a discussion of their validity. One excellent

presented in Mark, or only "simple" parables, such as the unmerciful servant or the good Samaritan? To recapitulate the argument advanced by Jülicher and adopted by many others: in the "complex" parables are to be found a number of metaphors (or tropes); these, then, are the parables which are allegorical (or tropical) and therefore difficult to comprehend; it follows that Jesus would *not* have uttered them since his purpose could not have been deliberately to conceal his meaning from the simple people. An interpretation of a parable can likewise be recognized as inauthentic if it is a detailed, point-by-point explanation.

A word of caution is called for. It may seem obvious to say that no one today can answer a question of the kind posed by Jülicher with absolute certainty; such historical knowledge is simply beyond our recovery. Yet the assuredness with which Jülicher and others more recently have answered the question negatively shows that a caveat is not unnecessary. Quite apart from the historical problem, however, Jülicher's literary description of the parables itself greatly needs to be reexamined; it is by no means without inaccuracies. Thus two aspects of Jülicher's thesis may be distinguished: the literary analysis of the parables' structure, and the historical question as to their genuineness. A distinction should be maintained, also, between the parables themselves and the interpretations sometimes appended to them in the Gospels.

In response to the literary aspect of Jülicher's thesis, it must in the first place be reiterated that *all* parables are non-literal or tropical. The parable that has only a literal level of meaning does not exist. Therefore no distinction can be made among the Synoptic parables in this respect.

In the second place, as was said earlier, a composition which is tropical in its whole or macro-meaning may or may not have tropes in its constituent or micro-meanings; nevertheless, there is no difference in the psychological process involved in discerning the tropical meaning of the parable in either case. The process is always the same: the hearer apprehends the literal meaning of the story and then perceives that this in turn suggests a further, tropical meaning. Indeed, the mental process of apprehending the tropical meaning in individual words and across a whole narrative is, again, precisely the same. (See Chapter 2, Section C above.) Thus a narrative that has a number of tropes in the small meanings is no more incomprehensible than a narrative that does not. Once the constituent or micro-meanings are apprehended, the meaning of the whole emerges; or, conversely, once the whole or macro-meaning is apprehended, the meanings of the parts fall into place. We cannot, then, consign those parables having several tropes to inauthenticity merely on the grounds that they are especially difficult to comprehend, since they are not.

---

study of the Synoptic use of parables is that of Jack Dean Kingsbury, *The Parables of Jesus in Matthew 13: A Study in Redaction-Criticism* (Richmond, Va.: John Knox, 1969).

This having been said, however, it must be added in the third place that there is in fact little difference in the number of tropes in the so-called simple and the so-called complex parables. It is not necessary that this be so; it simply happens to be the case—as a few examples will suffice to demonstrate. Following is a brief analysis of four parables. In the Gospels, one is followed by a long, detailed interpretation; one is followed by a short, summary interpretation; one is preceded by a question which provides the clue to its interpretation; and one is given no interpretation at all. Yet, as will be seen, the *parables themselves* differ little in the number of tropes in the constituent meanings. Of *all* of these parables, it is possible to give both a brief interpretation of the whole and an extensive interpretation of the parts.

The first example, the weeds among the wheat (Mt 13:24–30) is followed by a point-by-point explanation (vss. 36–43). In the parable itself, the wheat and the weeds stand for the righteous and the wicked among men; the harvest for the coming of the kingdom; the winnowing for separation or judgment; and the fire for the final punishment. From these constituent meanings, the hearer apprehends the meaning of the whole: that the righteous and the wicked are allowed to dwell together in the world until the end of this age, when they will be divided at the judgment.

The second example, the unmerciful servant (Mt 18:23–34), is followed by a brief explanation which summarizes the whole parable: "So also my heavenly Father will do to every one of you, if you do not forgive your brothers from your heart" (vs. 35). Nevertheless, it is also possible to give a more extended, detailed interpretation of this story. The king stands for God; his servants for men; the debts for moral transgressions; the settling of accounts for judgment; and imprisonment for punishment. It is out of these constituent meanings that the whole meaning emerges: that God will forgive us in the measure in which we forgive our fellow man.

The third example, the good Samaritan (Lk 10:30–37), is introduced by the lawyer's question, "And who is my neighbor?" (vs. 29), in which the meaning of the parable is implied. In this narrative, the priest and Levite represent officials of the established religion; the Samaritan those who, it is thought, stand outside the circle of God's people; and the wounded man, anyone in need. From these constituent meanings, the meaning of the whole parable becomes clear: that it is not official religiosity, but the doing of the concrete deed of love for the neighbor, that fulfills the law of God.

The fourth example, the barren fig tree (Lk 13:6–9), is not accompanied by an interpretation of any sort. Yet it is evident that the owner of the fig tree stands for God; the tree itself for Israel; and the fruit which it fails to bear for justice and righteousness. The meaning of the whole parable is that, though Israel has failed to produce righteousness, it will nevertheless be spared destruction for a time and given a last chance to repent.

These brief analyses of the parables may also be stated conversely. If the discursive effect of the weeds among the wheat is to teach that good and evil persons will co-exist until the day of judgment, then it *follows* that the wheat and the weeds stand for the righteous and the wicked, the harvest for the close of this age, the winnowing for judgment, and the fire for punishment. If the discursive effect of the unmerciful servant is to exhort us to forgive others as God forgives us, then it follows that the king stands for God, the servants for man, the debts for sins, and imprisonment for punishment. If the discursive effect of the good Samaritan is to show that God's will is not mere membership—not even status—in the official religion, but only the deed of love for the neighbor, then it follows that the priest and Levite represent those who are officially religious, the Samaritan those who are not, and the wounded man those in need. If the discursive effect of the barren fig tree is to state that Israel has been unrighteous but will be spared destruction for a time, then it follows that the owner stands for God, the tree for Israel, the fruit for righteousness, the destruction for the final punishment.[7]

There is, then, little difference in the number of tropes in the component or micro-meanings in these parables. Naturally, longer parables are apt to have more tropes than those that are shorter; but the difference is negligible. The parables, then, cannot be distinguished on the grounds that some have "many points" while others have "one point." In fact, all are made up of constituent meanings comprising the meaning of the whole.[8] It is, indeed, more accurate and helpful to speak of the meaning of the whole parable and of its constituent meanings than of "one point" and "many points"; while this suggested category may not dispel all difficulties in the interpretation of individual parables, it does set them in the proper framework. Again, in the case of every parable the discerning hearer perceives both the constituent meanings and the whole meaning, all of which are closely interrelated. In the case of every parable it is possible to give both a detailed interpretation of the component parts and a summary interpretation of the whole. Therefore the assertion that some parables can be judged inauthentic merely on the grounds that they are "complex" is unfounded. All the Synoptic parables, which happen to be quite alike in this respect, have equal claim to authenticity. This is not to maintain—as should by now be clear—that all the Synoptic parables, or their interpretations, are in fact authentic; but the question must be resolved on grounds other than the "complex"/"simple" distinction.

7. The thesis that there may be tropes in the constituent meanings remains correct even if one proposes a different interpretation of the original parable. As the large tropical meaning is modified, so are the tropes in the small meanings; they are not thereby altogether eliminated. See below, on Dodd's and Jeremias' reconstructions of the meaning of the parables of the weeds among the wheat and the fish-net.

8. The presence of tropes in the constituent meanings in many parables has, of course, already been demonstrated by a number of interpreters, notably Fiebig, *Altjüdische Gleichnisse* and *Die Gleichnisreden Jesu*; Black, "Parables as Allegory"; and Brown, "Parable and Allegory."

To observe that there are tropes in the constituent meanings of the parables is by no means to impugn their integrity.[9] It is surely not to say that they are fragmented or incoherent. In any artistic construct there is no reason why there cannot be component parts which are related in such a way as to form a unified and harmonious whole, or a composition having coherence. The world abounds in such objects in both the fine and practical arts—paintings, architectural structures, musical compositions—as anyone can readily perceive who has eyes to see and ears to hear. In any *good* allegory, including the allegorical parable, the component parts are well interrelated on the literal level (and thus we have a good story), as well as on the tropical level which it suggests. It is, of course, possible in a bad artistic construct—for example, in any unsuccessful allegory or parable—that the constituent parts be poorly interrelated; indeed it is largely because of such incoherence that the structure is an inferior one. What is important is that the distinction here is that between a good and a poor tropical composition, not that between an allegory and a parable.

To say that in an allegory the elements point primarily outside and only secondarily to one another, resulting in incoherence, whereas in a parable they point primarily to one another and only secondarily outside, resulting in coherence, is quite inaccurate.[10] What is meant, of course, is that there are tropes in the individual words in allegories, but not in parables. This misunderstanding needs to be unraveled. To begin with, all words, regardless of the kind of speech in which they appear, point outside themselves; it is their very nature to do so. By definition, a word is a sound which points to something (outside itself) and thus is meaningful. Similarly, all literary compositions as a whole refer to realities outside themselves. What occurs when we have the phenomenon of tropical meaning, as explained earlier, is that the word points to a thing (the literal meaning), and that thing in turn points to another thing (the tropical meaning). (See the description of metaphor in Chapter 2, Section C above.) This double reference always occurs across the macro-meaning, and sometimes also in the micro-meanings, in every tropical composition, which is to say in every allegory and in every parable without exception. It has been shown that it does in fact occur in both the whole and the constituent meanings in the Synoptic parables—and that their artistic integrity is not thereby damaged. Again, no distinction can be made in this respect between allegory and parable.

To be sure, not every word in a parable is a trope. Only those words which in context suggest further meaning are to be understood tropically. In the good Samaritan, for example, the four characters are unmistakably tropical, but not the town of Jericho, or the beast, or the inn. In the unmerciful

---

9. Via, *Parables*, 24–25, among others, regards the presence of tropes in micro-meanings as destructive of a parable's aesthetic unity.

10. See Via, *Parables*, 4–8, 24–25.

servant, the king and the servant are tropical, but not the servant's wife and children. The interpreter can often discern without too much difficulty which micro-meanings are intended tropically and which only literally, especially when these are taken in conjunction with the macro-meaning. Absolute certainty, it must be admitted, is not possible in every case. To see tropes where there are none is, of course, what is generally meant by "allegorizing." It is against this modern interpreters, beginning with Jülicher, have reacted. It is true, as comparison of the Synoptics shows, that the tradition sometimes added tropes as a way of adapting the parables to new situations, and it is one of the exegete's tasks to identify these. Insofar as exegetes reject the adding of tropes (in the parables), or the finding of tropes (in interpretations) where they do not exist, their position is correct. When they go on from there to conclude that there are never any tropes at all in the constituent meanings of parables, however, their position becomes incorrect.

It does not follow from what has been said that all the Synoptic parables are equally easy to comprehend. This is surely not the case. The parable of the sower, if heard without any interpretation, would be difficult; the parable of the prodigal son would be considerably easier; most parables would fall somewhere between these two extremes. How readily a parable may be interpreted depends partly on how natural—that is to say, how obvious to the hearer—are the tropical or suggested meanings (in both the parts and the whole), and partly on how well known to the hearer are the communal tropes of the Semitic tradition.

A few examples may show some differences in natural meaning. Good and bad fish, or wheat and weeds, quite obviously suggest good and evil things respectively, or the righteous and the wicked, and so these metaphors are fairly easy to interpret. It was said above that the sowing of seed suggests the dissemination of a thing; while this is true, it is not absolutely clear that what is disseminated is the word, as in the sower. The image can certainly suggest such a thing, and this meaning is quite natural, but it is not obvious, and so this metaphor is more difficult to interpret. As for communal tropes, that the figure of a father or master suggests God is apparent only to those acquainted to some extent with the Jewish or Christian traditions. Similarly, that the harvest and fire suggest the final judgment and punishment is evident only to those who have some knowledge, however elementary, of eschatological or apocalyptic thought. It might be pointed out, too, that synecdoches are more transparent than metaphors. For example, it is quite evident that the rich man, in the parable of the rich man and Lazarus, suggests all those who have an abundance of worldly goods but whose lives are devoid of moral quality. This is so because in synecdoche there is more similarity than dissimilarity between the two things compared, whereas in metaphor there is more dissimilarity than similarity.

While there are differences in the degree of difficulty with which the various parables can be understood, these differences are not owing to the number of tropes in their constituent meanings. It is not how many tropes a parable has, but how obvious are the natural meanings in both the small and the large tropical units, that determines how easy or how difficult it will be to comprehend. The flawed contrast between "simple" and "complex" parables, then, has little or nothing to do with the sometimes mysterious character of these speeches.

The historical aspect of Jülicher's thesis, that concerning the genuineness of the parables, must at last be addressed. The question posed by Jülicher might be recast in terms such as these: would Jesus have employed only those parables the meaning of which is obvious on first hearing, or would he also have employed parables which must be pondered in order to be understood? A definitive answer to the question, again, is simply not attainable. The most that can be said is that how one answers depends largely on certain presuppositions.

If we presume that when Jesus pronounced the parables an explanation of some kind was at times provided, then we may reasonably conclude that he employed parables which, when they appear alone, are somewhat difficult to comprehend. The explanation, it may be supposed, was provided by the situation which was its context, or by the question or discussion preceding the parable, or by an explicit interpretation following the parable. The problem, on this supposition, is easily solved.

If, on the other hand, we presume that all the parables were necessarily uttered by Jesus without any accompanying explanation, then how we answer the query depends on how we regard the "difficult" parables. If we view them as did Jülicher, that is, as absolute mysteries, then of course we will answer negatively. If, however, we view them as did Lagrange, that is, as intended to pique the curiosity of the listener, to lead him to reflect, perhaps to repent, then we may well answer positively. On this supposition, the question has to be put to each parable individually, whether by itself it could be understood by a hearer who was acquainted with the communal Semitic tropes, and who was willing to meditate on its meaning.

A separate question is that concerning the genuineness of the detailed explanations appended to some parables. The following are usually included in lists of such interpretations: those attached to the parables of the sower (Mk 4:1–9,13–20; Mt 13:1–9,18–23; Lk 8:4–8,11–15), the weeds among the wheat (Mt 13:24–30,36–43), and the fish-net (Mt 13:47–50), the first two of which are the most detailed; and those attached to the parables of the two sons (Mt 21:28–32), the lost sheep (Lk 15:3–7; Mt 18:12–14), and the lost coin (Lk 15:8–10), which are detailed, but less so than the first two.

To begin with the less detailed interpretations: there is no reason not to regard the Matthean explanation of the parable of the two sons as authentic (except for the reference to John the Baptist in the last verse). The Lukan interpretations of the twin parables of the lost sheep and the lost coin may also be taken as authentic (though the Matthean explanation of the former is no doubt secondary).[11] Then, the interpretations that are somewhat detailed can be and probably are genuine.

As for the more detailed interpretations: the Markan explanation of the sower will be treated in the following chapter. The Matthean explanation of the weeds among the wheat was very likely added by Matthew on the model of the interpretation of the sower, which he clearly took over with its parable from Mark; and the explanation of the fish-net was probably added by Matthew on the model of the explanation of the weeds among the wheat, since it is a summary of the latter part of that explanation. According to Jeremias, this conclusion is corroborated by the peculiarly Matthean vocabulary of these two interpretations.[12] The analogy with the Markan treatment of the sower, and the vocabulary, are the two decisive arguments against the authenticity of these interpretations.

According to both Dodd and Jeremias, a further argument against their authenticity is that they miss the meaning of the parables, which these scholars regard as genuine. Dodd believes that the weeds among the wheat originally taught that the kingdom comes with the ministry of Jesus, and is not delayed merely because there are sinners in Israel; and that the fish-net originally taught that the disciples, fishers of men, would appeal to persons of every type, who would then distinguish themselves by their different responses to the demands of discipleship.[13] Jeremias believes that the pair of parables originally stressed the need for patience and intended to teach that God would bring in his own time of separation.[14] Matthew, of course, presents these parables as a lesson teaching that there are good and evil men—presumably in the Church—and that the evil should not be removed before the last judgment, which is described as a future apocalyptic event.

Against Dodd and Jeremias, however, it must be said that it is not *because* the interpretation of the weeds among the wheat (and of its companion, the fish-net) is a point-by-point explanation that it is inauthentic. Whatever the original meaning of the parable may have been, the Matthean explanation is by no means a complete misreading; at the very least it correctly interprets the wheat and weeds as good and evil men, the harvest as the coming of the kingdom, and the winnowing as a separation or judgment. Indeed, the explanations of Dodd and Jeremias require the same interpretations! At

11. The Synoptic explanations of these three parables are not discussed at any length by either Dodd or Jeremias. However, Dodd, *Parables*, appears to regard the interpretation of the two sons as genuine (p. 93); he is not certain as to the genuineness of the Lukan explanations of the lost sheep and the lost coin, though he brings forward no compelling arguments against it (pp. 91–92). Jeremias, *Parables*, seems to view all of these interpretations as original (the latter two only in their Lukan version) (pp. 125, 38–40, 132–36).

12. Jeremias, *Parables*, 81–85.

13. Dodd, *Parables*, 147–52.

14. Jeremias, *Parables*, 81–85, 224–27.

issue is simply the question whether the parable belongs in the setting of Jesus' ministry or of the Church. That is to say, *specifically* are the righteous and unrighteous persons Israelites, Jesus' disciples, or Christians; and do the coming of the kingdom and the judgment occur as the eschatological event during or soon after Jesus' ministry, or as the apocalyptic event at some future time? However one interprets the whole tropical meaning, it must be acknowledged that there are tropes also in its constituent meanings. Then, it is not by its setting-out of the detailed tropical meanings that Matthew's interpretation can be recognized as inauthentic.

In the Synoptic Gospels the very detailed explanations are few, and in at least two cases are probably not part of the original utterance of the parable by Jesus (if, that is, the parables themselves are authentic); that is most likely because such point-by-point explanations are often unnecessary. In many cases either the question or discussion preceding the parable, or a summary interpretation following the parable, is sufficient; the interpretations of the constituent parts are easily filled in by the hearer. In other cases an interpretation that is only somewhat detailed will do. In some cases no interpretation at all is required; the meaning of the parable is evident, both in its whole and in its parts. It is highly probable that Matthew's motive in providing the interpretations of the weeds among the wheat and the fish-net was not to elucidate these parables, but to imitate the Markan pattern of public pronouncement and private explanation. One final point must be added: to say that it does not go back to Jesus is not to say that such an interpretation totally misrenders the meaning of the parable. It may interpret it quite correctly, at least in its broad lines, while of course also allowing for some adaptations that would enhance the relevance of the parable for the evangelist and his readers (if, again, the parable itself is genuine); this seems to be the case with Matthew's interpretations of the weeds among the wheat and the fish-net.

C. THE HISTORICAL QUESTION

A question of great interest in the study of parables is whether or not individual parables and their explanations are authentic words of Jesus. A distinction relevant to this question is that between the *meaning* and the *structure of meaning* of a literary work. (This is the distinction referred to frequently but somewhat less correctly as "content" and "form.")[15] The matter of authenticity has to do with the former, and not the latter. That is to say, it is the meaning, or, quite simply, what the parable or its interpretation *says*, that should be the central consideration in a judgment concerning its authenticity; the structure of meaning, or how the parable or its interpretation is *constructed*, is not a factor of significance. Such questions

---

15. On these terms, see La Drière, "Form," "Classification, Literary," and "Structure, Sound, and Meaning."

as how many tropes a parable has; or whether an interpretation states only the whole meaning ("one point") or also the constituent meanings ("many points") of the parable; or in what way parable and interpretation differ as literary constructs, have little or no bearing on the assessment of historicity. Certainly it is unsound to base the judgment concerning genuineness on a faulty parable/allegory contrast; structurally, there is nothing defective in either the parables or their interpretations as they appear in the Synoptic Gospels.

The investigation of historicity involves what are really two interrelated tasks, an examination of the interpretation by itself, and an examination of the parable or the parable-plus-interpretation. Of the interpretation, it should be asked whether it seems truly to render the meaning of the parable, that is, to express the meaning which arises naturally out of the parable itself. Of both the parable and its interpretation, such questions should be asked as whether it departs from the more convincing version in another of the canonical Gospels or some other source such as the Gospel of Thomas; whether it seems to reflect the conditions (including language) of Jesus' ministry or those of the early Church; and whether it coheres with the eschatological and ethical teaching of Jesus derived from other Synoptic material. In short, the usual criteria employed to identify authentic material in the Synoptics are to be employed here also, to determine whether the composition is an authentic parable, a creation of the Church, or a modification by the Church of an authentic parable.[16]

Such an examination, it is important to observe, is an analysis of meaning, not of structure. It is, moreover, by and large an *historical* analysis of meaning. Except for the first question asked of the interpretation, all of the questions suggested above are of an historical order. The decision as to whether a parable and its interpretation are genuine is, in the final analysis, made almost entirely on historical grounds (meaning) rather than on grounds of literary structure (structure of meaning). The central question always is, could Jesus, sometime during his ministry, have uttered this parable with the meaning attached to it in this Gospel?

When all is said and done, however, the results obtained by such an investigation are far from assured. The variety of interpretations and reconstructions of the "original" parables put forward by scholars—among which it is often impossible to choose with any confidence—attests to the difficulty of the historical task. Above all, however, it attests to the difficulty of interpreting tropical language with exactness and certainty; as Morton Smith has said, there are enough differences among modern interpretations of the parables to support the ancient view that they are mysterious things.[17]

16. An interesting example of the application of the criterion of "coherence" to two parables (the prodigal son and the weeds among the wheat) is found in Charles Edwin Carlston, "A *Positive* Criterion of Authenticity?" *BR* 7 (1962) 33–44.

17. Morton Smith, "Comments on Taylor's Commentary on Mark," *HTR* 48 (1955) 31.

4

THE MARKAN THEORY OF PARABLES

The research on parables since the nineteenth century has been directed mainly toward the ultimate goal of explaining the theory of parables in Mark 4: that is the real object of interest. No study of the parables would be complete that did not include an examination of the Gospel of Mark. These final chapters will therefore attempt to describe Mark's parable theory, and the broader theme of which that theory is a part, the motif of mystery.

One of the best ways of entering into the redaction of Mark's Gospel is via the author's notion of parables. A correct understanding of the crucial parable chapter, Mark 4, sheds light on the entire Gospel and its purpose. The importance of rightly perceiving Mark's view of parables can hardly be overestimated.

A. THE MARKAN PARABLE DISCOURSE (4:1–34)

The Parable of the Sower Publicly Pronounced (vss. 1–9)
The Purpose of Parables (vss. 10–12)
The Parable of the Sower Privately Explained (vss. 13–20)
Wisdom Sayings (vss. 21–25)
The Similitude of the Growing Seed (vss. 26–29)
The Similitude of the Mustard Seed (vss. 30–32)
Conclusion: The Use of Parables (vss. 33–34)

Most studies of the Markan parable discourse have been form-critical analyses. They have attempted to get behind the Markan chapter to the original meaning of its component parts (outlined above) in Jesus' ministry. The presupposition of such studies is that the Markan theory of parables, as it stands, is difficult and offensive. To recapitulate: Mark has, in the first place, mistaken the parables for allegories; he therefore thinks they are mysterious, and must be explained. He reveals his error by appending to the parable of the sower a private explanation which is allegorical (that is, point-by-point), and therefore secondary. But what is worse, he has Jesus state that he used parables for the purpose of excluding those outside the circle of disciples from understanding, conversion, and forgiveness—as Hunter says, as if he employed parables deliberately to befuddle the people.[1] F. C. Grant summarized his own opinion and that of many others when he characterized

---

1. Archibald Macbride Hunter, *The Gospel According to Saint Mark*, Torch Bible Commentaries (London: SCM Press, 1949) 55.

Mark's theory as perverse.[2] But once the form critic recovers the original meaning of each unit of this chapter in the teaching of Jesus, it becomes quite acceptable. Such restoration is the major task of the exegete.

It is a question whether this interpretation of the Markan concept of parables does justice to the thought of the evangelist. The present study is a fresh attempt to understand the parable theory just as it stands in the Gospel. It is a redactional analysis which has as its purpose simply to describe what lies before us with accuracy. It is also an attempt to situate the Markan chapter in its religio-historical setting, that is, to investigate the Semitic background of the motifs which appear in the chapter. Such an investigation cannot, of course, show that the notion of parables in Mark goes back to the historical Jesus, nor is it here undertaken for that purpose. It can, however, illuminate the Markan theory itself.

The entire Markan passage (4:1-34) is a lesson on how to hear the word about the kingdom spoken in parables. This is made evident by the frequent occurrence of such words as *speak, hear, kingdom,* and *parable. Kingdom* appears three times (vss. 11,26,30); *parable* eight times (vss. 2,10,11,13, 30,33,34). And we read: "Listen!" (vs. 3); "He who has ears to hear, let him hear" (vss. 9,23); "The sower sows the word" (vs. 14); "those who hear the word" (vs. 18, and throughout vss. 15-20); "Take heed what you hear" (vs. 24); and finally, "With many such parables he spoke the word to them, as they were able to hear it" (vs. 33). The first task of the exegete, then, is to discern what precisely this section says about listening to the proclamation of the kingdom in parables. This can best be done by an examination of each component part in turn, and of the parallels to the Markan motifs in the OT and Jewish literature.

The Purpose of Parables (vss. 10-12)[3]

The passage distinguishes sharply between the disciples and non-disciples.[4] To the disciples alone is given the secret of the kingdom; all others

2. Frederick C. Grant, "The Gospel According to St. Mark," *IDB* VII, 700.

3. For a discussion of the theory in Mk 4:10-12 see, in addition to the commentaries and monographs on parables listed in the bibliography, the following: M.-J. Lagrange, "Le but des paraboles d'après l'Evangile selon Saint Marc," *RB* n.s. 7 (1910) 5-35; T. A. Burkill, "The Cryptology of Parables in St. Mark's Gospel," *NovT* 1 (1956) 246-62; W. Manson, "The Purpose of the Parables: A Re-Examination of St. Mark iv.10-12," *ExpT* 68 (1956-57) 132-35; Edward F. Siegman, "Teaching in Parables (Mk 4,10-12; Lk 8,9-10; Mt 13,10-15)," *CBQ* 23 (1961) 161-81; T. A. Burkill, Ch. 5: "Parables and the Secret," *Mysterious Revelation: An Examination of the Philosophy of St. Mark's Gospel* (Ithaca, N.Y.: Cornell University Press, 1963) 96-116.

4. The term *hoi exō* occurs elsewhere in the NT only in the Pauline letters, where it refers to those outside the Christian community (1 Cor 5:12,13; Col 4:5; 1 Thes 4:12). Sirach speaks of non-Jews as outsiders (*hoi ektos*: Prol.). According to Henry Barclay Swete, *The Gospel According to St Mark* (3rd ed.; New York: Macmillan, 1909) 76; Lagrange, "Le but des

are taught in mysterious parables. The reason: so that those outside will not understand, repent, and be forgiven. The teaching, as Morton Smith has said, is clear enough.[5] It is a stark doctrine of determinism: God's plan is that some people be excluded from salvation, and Jesus used the parables as an instrument to that end. This effect of the parables is understood as a fulfillment of the prophecy of Isa 6:9–10.[6]

The purpose of the statement is to show that all history is in God's control. It was an historical reality that many people—indeed the Jewish nation as a whole—had rejected the teaching of Jesus and the preaching of the apostles. The early Christian thinkers had somehow to account for that. They explained it quite straightforwardly with the doctrine that such a course of events had been the will of God (see the same idea in Rom 9:18–29; 10:16–21; 11:7–10; Jn 12:37–41; Acts 28:25–28).

Only one further point need be made. There is some question as to whether it is the coming kingdom or the parabolic speech that is mysterious.[7] The answer is that it is both, as the passage itself shows. We have on the one hand the expression "the secret of the kingdom of God," and on the other the inability of the hearers, even the disciples, to understand the parable of the sower. The coming of the kingdom is a mystery. So is the indirect mode of speech called parable. The two have been skillfully combined by the evangelist or the tradition before him. But much more needs to be said about this twofold mystery; the two questions, what precisely constitutes the "secret of the kingdom," and in what sense the parables may be said to be

---

paraboles," 26; and Siegman, "Teaching in Parables." 173. the word "outsiders" (*ha hîsônîm*) became a standard rabbinic term for Gentiles or for Jews less instructed than the Pharisees. C. E. B. Cranfield, *The Gospel According to Saint Mark*, Cambridge Greek Testament Commentary (Cambridge: Cambridge University Press, 1959; reprinted, with supplementary notes, 1963) 154, arguing against the theory that the term *hoi exō* shows the influence of the Hellenistic mystery cults, says that no instance of its use in classical Greek to refer to "the uninitiated" has been brought forward; several words were regularly used for that (*amuētos, atelestos, abakcheutos. behēlos*).

5. Smith, "Comments on Taylor's Commentary," 30.

6. One well known attempt to mitigate the severity of Mk 4:10–12 is the thesis of Manson, *Teaching*, 77–80, that the *hina* is a mistranslation of the Aramaic particle *d*, which occurs in the Targum version of the quotation from Isaiah on which Mk 4:12 seems to be dependent; it should have been rendered *hoi*. For a summary of other attempts to show that the *hina* is a mistranslation, see Vincent Taylor, *The Gospel According to St. Mark* (2nd ed.; London: Macmillan, 1966) 257. For a discussion of the Aramaic behind the Markan Greek quotation, and a refutation of Manson's thesis, see Matthew Black, *An Aramaic Approach to the Gospels and Acts* (3rd ed.; Oxford: Clarendon Press, 1967) 211–16.

7. The question is raised, for example, by Raymond E. Brown, *The Semitic Background of the Term "Mystery" in the New Testament* (Philadelphia: Fortress Press, 1968) 34. (This is substantially a reprint of his articles, "The Pre-Christian Semitic Concept of 'Mystery,'" *CBQ* 20 [1958] 417–43; and "The Semitic Background of the New Testament *Mystērion*," Parts I and II, *Bib* 39 [1958] 426–48 and 40 [1959] 70–87.) Brown maintains that "mystery" here refers to God's plan of salvation and has no intrinsic relation to parables.

mysterious, will be discussed in Chapter 5, following the exegesis of all the relevant passages.

It has been said that the statement on the purpose of parables in vss. 10–12 contradicts other parts of this chapter which call for a right hearing of the parables, namely the parable of the sower and its explanation; the rebuke to the disciples for not understanding the parable; the injunction to listen in vss. 3, 9, and 23; the sayings in vss. 21–25; and the conclusion in vs. 33: "And in many such parables he spoke the word to them, as they were able to hear."[8] The inconsistency, it is said, reveals the composite character of the chapter. It would be more correct to say that the whole chapter is properly understood only when the statement on the purpose of parables is taken together with these other units. The chapter may well be a composite, but what Mark has made of it is not so much a clumsy patchwork as a finely balanced piece.

The Parable of the Sower and Its Interpretation (vss. 1–9,13–20)[9]

Whether the parable of the sower is an allegory, and whether the Markan interpretation is secondary, are two questions which should be kept distinct. The first and easier question has been answered in earlier chapters; the parable is an allegory, an extended metaphor in narrative form. Regardless of what its original setting and meaning may have been, that it always had both a literal and a metaphorical level of meaning is certain. The second question is vastly more difficult. Before it is addressed, a redactional analysis will be made of the parable and interpretation in Mark 4.

In this Gospel, the parable of the sower begins "Listen!" (vs. 3).[10] The word recalls the introduction to the *Shemaʿ*, "Hear, O Israel" (Dt 6:4). (Three OT *meŝālîm* begin with a similar injunction: Jgs 9:7; Isa 28:23; Ezek 20:47. Cf. *1 Enoch* 37:1.) In Mark the word warns the hearer to be attentive both because what follows is of great import, and because it will be conveyed indirectly in a parable. The point is reiterated in the conclusion: "He who has ears to hear, let him hear" (vs. 9; cf. Dt 29:4; Isa 6:10; Jer 5:21; Ezek 3:27; 12:2).

8. So, for example, B. Harvie Branscomb, *The Gospel of Mark*, The Moffatt New Testament Commentary (New York: Harper, 1937) 77; and Nineham, *St Mark*, 136.

9. On the Markan parables, especially the sower, see, in addition to the commentaries and monographs on parables listed in the bibliography, the following articles: Nils A. Dahl, "The Parables of Growth," *ST* 5 (1952) 132–66; Augustin George, "Le sens de la parabole des semailles (Mc., IV, 3–9 et parallèles)," *SacPag* 2 (1959) 163–69; Black, "Parables as Allegory"; Brown, "Parable and Allegory"; C. H. Cave, "The Parables and the Scriptures," *NTS* 11 (1964–65) 374–87; and Gerhardsson, "Parable of the Sower."

10. The word "Listen!" is lacking here in the Gospels of Matthew, Luke, and Thomas. Gerhardsson, "Parable of the Sower," 189, sees a parallel in *2 Esdras* 9:30ff., where the injunction, "Hear me, O Israel," introduces a parable using the image of seed for the law.

On the literal level, the parable tells the story of a sower scattering seed, some of which falls on poor soil and dies, some of which falls on good soil and lives and grows and bears fruit. On the metaphorical level, according to Mark's Gospel, it exhorts the hearer to receive in faith and keep with steadfastness the word that is disseminated. As it stands in the Gospel, of course, the parable has two historical settings. Mark tells of Jesus' preaching to a Jewish audience, and so the "word" is Jesus' proclamation of the coming kingdom (cf. 2:2); but Mark himself is addressing his own readers, and so the "word" is also the Church's proclamation of the Christian message (cf. Lk 1:2; Acts 4:4; 1 Cor 1:18).

If the statement in vss. 10–12 emphasizes the absolute control of God over man's destiny, the parable of the sower and its explanation stress the need for man to respond to the proclamation of the kingdom. The success of the proclamation depends as much on the hearer as on the speaker. It is incumbent on man to resist the attacks of Satan, "tribulation or persecution," "the cares of the world, and the delight in riches, and the desire for other things"; and to "hear the word and accept it and bear fruit" (vss. 15–20). The statement on the purpose of parables treats of God's sovereignty and predestination, the parable and its explanation treat of man's role and responsibility.

The sower is placed at the beginning of this collection because it is the most important parable in the Gospel. That is because it is the key to understanding all the other parables. It is basic because the seed that is sown is the word spoken by Jesus; but it is only in parables that Jesus spoke the word (vss. 11,33–34); then, in a sense, the seed stands for the parables. Thus it is a parable on the right hearing of parables. That is why Jesus says to his disciples, "Do you not understand this parable? How then will you understand all the parables?" (vs. 13). The very question, it should be noted, shows the understanding of parables to be a possibility.

Although the intention of this chapter is to provide a redactional rather than a form-critical analysis of certain aspects of Mark's Gospel, an exception will now be made to this general approach, and some remarks tendered on the vexed question of the authenticity of the sower and its Markan explanation. This brief discussion will provide one example of the application of the theory outlined in the preceding chapters. A line will be drawn between the literary and the historical considerations. It should be restated at the outset, however, that even the best literary theory cannot dispel all of the difficulties which arise in the interpretation of any particular parable; the following discussion will therefore illustrate as much the limits of literary theory as the possibilities it provides for sound exegesis. It will show what literary analysis cannot tell us as well as what it can tell us about the original meaning of a parable.

The genuineness of the parable of the sower itself (vss. 1–9) has not often been brought into question. According to Black,[11] the Greek gives evidence of translation of an Aramaic source, which makes possible, and perhaps even probable, the parable's authenticity. Moreover, comparison with the very similar version in the Gospel of Thomas (9) shows that we have in Mark what must have been basically the original structure of the parable. But what Jesus intended it to mean, or whether the Markan explanation is authentic, is virtually impossible to determine.

First, the literary considerations: Interpreting a parable, as has been observed, involves two interrelated factors: apprehending its natural meaning, and being acquainted with the communal tropes which it employs. Each parable should be examined for suggested meaning, and this in the light of the tradition behind it.

The parable of the sower, as noted earlier, is perhaps the most difficult of all the Synoptic parables to comprehend. *That is not, however, because it is composed of a number of tropes, but because its natural meaning is not obvious.* Three basic interpretations have been proposed in recent exegesis: that the parable has to do with the kingdom, and speaks of the contrast between its none too promising beginnings and its final breaking-in with splendor, thus encouraging those with little hope; that it has to do with the labor of Jesus or his disciples, and speaks of the contrast between its present failure and its ultimate success, thus reassuring those beset with doubt; and that it has to do with the preaching of Jesus, and exhorts the audience to hear and do the word—as Mark would have it. Most other current interpretations are variations of these.[12] The question is, which of these meanings is suggested naturally by the parable itself?

All that can be said with certainty regarding the natural meaning of this parable is that it has to do with the incipience or the dissemination of something, which in part is frustrated and fails and in part goes on to succeed in a most impressive manner. The seed suggests something implanted or promulgated; the poor soil, loss; the good soil, gain. What cannot be known is what the seed stands for, that is, what it is which is being begun or disseminated and which partly goes to waste and partly produces a great yield. Each of the three interpretations of the parable summarized above is altogether natural and may be correct; there is no literary reason for discounting any one. Nothing one can glean from the parable itself points to a definitive choice.

11. Black, *Aramaic Approach*, 45.

12. For a summary of various interpretations see Taylor, *St. Mark*, 250–51; C. E. B. Cranfield, "St. Mark 4.1–34," Part I, *SJT* 4 (1951) 398–414, esp. 399–405; and Cranfield, *Saint Mark*, 150–51. For a review of the arguments against the authenticity of the Markan interpretation, and a rebuttal of each, see Cranfield, "St. Mark 4.1–34," 405–412; and Cranfield, *Saint Mark*, 158–61.

If the parable itself does not give the clue to its meaning, then it is sensible to ask next whether other sources can provide help by enlightening us as to a traditional or communal use of its basic trope. The image of seed appears in OT and Jewish writings as well as in other Synoptic passages; it is reasonable to inquire whether these parallels can illuminate the Markan metaphor.

In Jer 31:27-28, 2 Esdras 8:41-45, and the Matthean parable of the weeds among the wheat (Mt 13:24-30,36-43), the seed represents mankind. In 2 Esdras we read that just as "not all [the seeds] that have been sown will come up," so too "those who have been sown in the world will not all be saved" (vs. 41).

Elsewhere in the Synoptic Gospels, namely in the similitudes of the growing seed and the mustard seed (Mk 4:26-32; Mt 13:31-32; Lk 13:18-19), the seed stands for the kingdom.

The seed can also represent something sown in man.[13] A Jewish example exists in which the seed is God's law; 2 Esdras 9:31-37 begins: "For behold, I sow my law in you, and it shall bring forth fruit in you, and you shall be glorified through it for ever" (vs. 31). In 2 Esdras 4:28-32, the seed stands for evil, a grain of which was sown in Adam.

It may be concluded that Jesus' audience would not have known the meaning of the metaphor from a consistent use in the religious tradition familiar to them, or for that matter from the preaching of Jesus. As a survey of the literature shows, a number of natural meanings could be suggested by the image of seed. Thus no clue is provided us by the parallels of pre-Christian or early Christian times.

It is sometimes said that the parable of the sower should be interpreted in conformity with the two similitudes adjacent to it in the Markan parable chapter, those of the growing seed and the mustard seed (vss. 26-32); it would then be understood, like those, as a parable about the kingdom. It is likely, however, that these three parables were originally separate and were brought together later only because all employ the same basic image. In view of their probably distinct origins, and of the diverse meanings of the image in the tradition, each parable in Mark's chapter ought to be examined on its own terms, and interpreted according to its own suggested meaning.

It is not being maintained here that the Markan interpretation necessarily gives the original meaning of the parable; that thesis lies beyond the realm of what can be proven. What is being proposed is that the meaning stated in Mark is possibly the original one, that it has equal claim to correctness with the other two interpretations advanced in modern exegesis.

---

13. We find a precedent in the Greek literature; Socrates used the planting of seed as a metaphor for teaching or the communication of an idea (logos—Phaedrus 61; see Appendix). This suggests, not of course that the Socratic parable is the ancestor of the Markan one, but only that this tropical meaning is natural.

The view of the present study is that the Markan interpretation gives a very natural rendering of the parable, one which fits it perfectly. The hearer would have to be told that the parable as a whole has to do with hearing the word; but once so informed, he would have little difficulty in apprehending many of its constituent meanings. That the scattering of seed stands for the dissemination of the word; the ground for those among whom the word is broadcast; the poor and rich soil for those respectively who fail and who succeed in receiving and keeping the word; and the final yield of grain for righteousness—these are meanings that are derived quite naturally from the story. There is nothing in the broad lines of this interpretation that strains the sense of the reference in the parable itself. Even a simple, uneducated hearer of the kind that must have largely made up the audiences of Jesus would have been able to supply these constituent meanings, once he had perceived the whole meaning to be about the word.

There is yet further natural meaning that could have been suggested to a more sophisticated hearer, one who was willing and able to ruminate on the narrative. The birds who come and devour the first seed suggest an enemy, and one that is an outside agent, external to the earth. The rocky ground upon which the second seed falls suggests shallowness, a spontaneous but superficial response, the inability to survive hard times. The word "thorn" connotes something evil and injurious; thus the thorns among which the third seed falls suggest some pernicious thing in the very earth. The good soil in which the fourth seed falls and grows suggests the opposite of all these: resistance to attack from without, strength and endurance, the overcoming of difficulties from within. An intelligent hearer would be able to glean from the story such meanings as these, again if he initially understood the parable to be about the hearing of the word.

A number of other observations could be made which corroborate this interpretation. The figure of the sower appears briefly at the beginning of the parable, but only as the instrument for the scattering of the seed; he then disappears, and the parable narrates exclusively the outcome of the sowing according to the different kinds of soil on which the seed falls. This makes it probable that the sower is of little significance, and that the subject of the story is the seed and soil. If that is true, it seems more likely that the parable is about hearing the word than about the ministry of Jesus. The following points may be made regarding the seed and soil: As comparison with the parallel $me^{e}\check{s}\bar{a}lim$ (cited above) reveals, a distinctive feature of the parable of the sower is the amount of attention given to the various types of ground. All the other examples present a simple contrast between failure and success in producing a yield; only in this parable as it appears in both the Gospels of Mark and Thomas are four different kinds of earth described. This, too, would seem to suggest that the meaning of the parable lies in the differences in the ground. Furthermore, just as there are variations in the poor soil, so too there are variations in the good soil; some yields thirtyfold, some sixtyfold, some a hundredfold. This diversity would seem to imply many different recipients of the seed, on the "good" as well as the "bad" side, and gradation in the yield of grain. Finally, the dissimilarity in kinds of soil seems of more importance in the story than the lapse of time between the sowing and the bearing of fruit; this may signify that what matters is variation in the receiving of the seed rather than present failure and future success. None of these points could very well be taken into account if the parable is not about the word, but about the kingdom—for it is difficult to know in what sense it could be said that there is diversity in the coming of the kingdom of God.

To say all of this about the parable, however, is still not to arrive at the full meaning given in the interpretation found in Mark's Gospel (vss. 13–20). The difficulty which many exegetes express concerning the Markan explanation has to do with the detail with which it speaks of the three types of poor soil. The difficulty is understandable. It is really based, however, not on the fact that Mark's explanation is point-by-point, but on the fact that all of the meanings it states do not arise obviously out of the parable itself. The hearer, whether simple or sophisticated, would be hard put to know that the birds stand for Satan (vs. 15); the rocky ground for those hearers who fall away because of "tribulation or persecution" (vs. 17); and the thorns for "the cares of the world, and the delight in riches, and the desire for other things" (vs. 19). These meanings are hardly conspicuous. What a hearer could be expected to deduce, as observed earlier, is that the different types of poor soil suggest superficiality in general, a failure to nurture the word, to accept and observe it in the face of difficulties from without and within.

What the author of the interpretation (whoever he may have been) has done with the parable, however, is by no means a falsification of its meaning. With artful skill, he has delineated the psychological dispositions of various hearers who by their states of mind are led to one or another kind of action of a moral order. This the author has done in such a way that the description of each kind of hearer in the interpretation is quite suited to the description of each kind of soil in the parable. So once stated, these meanings, it must be said, fit the parable perfectly.

Incidentally, the inconsistency in the Markan interpretation, which speaks of the hearers sometimes as seed and sometimes as soil, is not a cogent argument against its correctness. To require perfect consistency here is to demand a rigorous logic which cannot be expected of what is, after all, folk literature. The shift from seed to soil does not at all damage the coherence of the interpretation.

If the Markan interpretation of the parable is the correct one, then there are at least two possibilities regarding the circumstances of its original pronouncement. One is that when Jesus uttered the parable, its meaning was indicated by a discussion concerning the word which constituted its context.[14] It may be that the parable as spoken by Jesus was simply about the contrast between two kinds of hearers, those who do not and those who do receive and keep the word; if so, then what Mark (or a predecessor) did was to refine without altering the meaning of the parable. This would explain whatever reflections there might be in the Markan explanation of the primitive Church's situation. Another possibility is that Jesus himself provided an explicit interpretation of the parable much like that given in the Gospel. As noted, there seems to have been ample precedent for such a method of teaching, judging from the OT and Jewish writings.

In either case, the parable was based on the apt metaphor which employs the image of seed for the word (as in Socrates' dialogue; see Appendix); this is close to the use of the image of seed for the law, as in 2 Esdras. This metaphor was combined with the idea of various kinds of hearers; as is well known, a good pre-Christian parallel to this notion is found in the Pirqe Aboth 5:21, where we have a māšāl on four types of hearers, or four types of students who sit at the feet of sages. This māšāl may have been familiar to many among Jesus' audience.

The Markan interpretation of the constituent meanings, it must be said, is correct only if the interpretation of the whole meaning is correct. If the macro-meaning differs from that given in Mark, then of course so do the micro-meanings.

Second, the historical considerations: The historical arguments often raised against the genuineness of the Markan explanation are these: that it changes the thrust of the parable from an eschatological to a psychological and hortative one; that its vocabulary is similar to that of the later NT epistolary literature and Acts; and that it presumes the situation of the early Church, when enough time would have elapsed for some Christians to apostatize under pressure of temptation or persecution.

Jeremias[15] has argued that the meaning stated in Mark cannot be original because it transforms the message of the parable from an eschatological one (about the coming kingdom) to a psychological one (about hearing the word). As the above observations have attempted to show, however, it is precisely the main point of the parable that is not clear from the parable itself. It can no more be demonstrated that the parable has to do with the kingdom than that it has to do with the word; both are equally possible. Jesus' teaching in general deals both with the proclamation of the coming kingdom of God and with man's response to that proclamation; this parable in particular could as well belong to the one as to the other aspect of his preaching.

The terms of the debate might at this point be clarified. It would be better to speak of the two alternative concerns of the parable as eschatology and

---

14. On this interpretation, the background to such a use of the term logos would be the prophetic literature.

15. Jeremias, Parables, 79, 150.

ethics, rather than eschatology and psychology. It was said earlier that rhetorical speech has as its purpose to convince, to persuade, to move to decision or action. To persuade the hearer to execute a moral decision or action is one of the many possible goals of rhetorical speech. To convince the hearer that the kingdom of God is at hand and that he must therefore repent is another. A parable might have an eschatological or an ethical, but not strictly speaking a psychological, purpose. A parable having an ethical aim could, however, describe the frame of mind, or the psychology, which would issue in a certain ethical choice. While the parable of the sower, according to Mark, describes people's attitudes, its *purpose* is not psychological but ethical.

The Markan explanation of this parable is hardly singular in respect to what it says. Notions of moral theology very similar to those expressed in the Markan interpretation are an important part of the teaching of both the OT prophets and Jesus. That God requires of man that he "bear fruit"—by which is meant justice and righteousness—is an Israelite and Jewish conviction of long duration, echoed in the Synoptic Gospels. In Isa 5:1–7 we read that the Lord's vineyard, which yielded only wild grapes, is Israel: "and he looked for justice, but behold, bloodshed; for righteousness, but behold, a cry!" (vs. 7b; cf. Jer 2:21; Ezek 19:10–14; Hos 10:1). Essentially the same metaphor appears in 2 *Esdras* 9:31–37, where the law sown in man is expected to yield fruit (vs. 31). It is also the basis for the Synoptic parable of the barren fig tree (Lk 13:6–9); and of the saying that "each tree is known by its own fruit" (Lk 6:44; cf. Mt 3:8–10; 7:16–20; 12:33–35; Lk 6:43–45). In all of these passages we have an exhortation to man to produce good works; the responsibility, he is told, lies with him.

A number of other Synoptic parables exhibit the same concern with moral attitude and action as the Markan version of the parable of the sower; they describe the characters' various psychological dispositions, which lead to an ethical decision of one kind or another. Such, to cite a few examples, are the parables of the prodigal son (Lk 15:11–32), the good Samaritan (Lk 10:30–37), the two sons (Mt 21:28–32), and the talents (Mt 25:14–30; Lk 19:12–27). The same injunction to have both a right attitude and right action is expressed in other teaching of Jesus, as for example in the sermon on the mount, especially in the six great antitheses (Mt 5:21–48) and the discussion of pious practices (Mt 6:1–18).

The conclusion to which these observations lead is that, in view of the teaching of the OT prophets and of Jesus himself, the parable of the sower could as well be an ethical exhortation on hearing the word as an eschatological revelation of the coming of the kingdom. The judgment as to the authenticity of Mark's explanation must then, in the final analysis, be based on the last two historical considerations: whether its vocabulary, and whether the conditions it presupposes, could belong to Jesus' ministry or only to the early Church. The evidence pro and con is extensively presented elsewhere; nothing further can be added here to the thorough discussions already available.[16] Since the arguments on either side fall short of conclusiveness, each interpreter must decide, without absolute certainty, on the answer to the central question: could Jesus have spoken this parable at some time during his ministry with the meaning attached to it in this Gospel?

Wisdom Sayings (vss. 21-25)

These verses consist of two pairs of parallel wisdom sayings (vss. 21-22, 24-25) joined by a connecting sentence (vs. 23).[17] The sayings constitute a commentary on both the statement in vss. 10-12 and the parable of the sower. They may indeed be said to reconcile the teaching in these two units, and are among the most important verses in the parable chapter.

The pair of sayings in vss. 21-22 explain further the mystery of the kingdom briefly mentioned in vs. 11. If the coming kingdom is presently hidden, that is only for a time; its full manifestation will occur in the future. But there may be a more specific meaning here. These verses perhaps intend to say that if the announcement of the coming of the kingdom is hidden in the parables, that is only so that the hearers may ponder them until their meaning is fully understood. The revelation is not completely hidden in these parables; it is meant to be brought to light by the hearers themselves. On this interpretation, these sayings teach the same lesson as the explanation of the parable of the sower.

That, in any case, is surely the meaning of the connecting vs. 23: "If any man has ears to hear, let him hear." This verse explicitly links the wisdom sayings to the parable of the sower (vs. 9). Again, the appeal to attentive listening signals both the importance and the indirectness of what is being said. It points, as Cranfield[18] has written, to the connection between the obliqueness of revelation and the need for personal decision in the matter of faith; the revelation of the kingdom is indirect *in order* to make faith possible, in order to give room for that personal decision.

The pair of sayings in vss. 24-25 certainly pursues the lesson in the interpretation of the parable of the sower. It teaches that the attentiveness which the hearer brings to a parable will be the measure of understanding he will receive from it—rather, the understanding given him will exceed his attentiveness. But if the hearer brings no attentiveness at all, even what little understanding he has will be taken from him.

16. See especially Dodd, *Parables*, 145-47; Jeremias, *Parables*, 77-79, 149-51; and the discussions of Cranfield cited above, n. 12.

17. On the parallelism of these wisdom sayings, see Burney, *Poetry of Our Lord*, 63-65, 71-74; and Taylor, *St. Mark*, 262.

18. Cranfield, *Saint Mark*, 165-66.

These sayings may be pressed even further to provide an explanation for the difficult yoking together of determinism and free will in this Markan chapter. They define a spiritual law at work in the preaching and hearing of the word. While man makes the initial decision to see or not to see, to hear or not to hear, God will assist him in that choice: "For to him who has will more be given; and from him who has not, even what he has will be taken away" (vs. 25). One might say that God confirms the believer in his belief, and the unbeliever in his disbelief—thus the interplay between the will of God and the will of man. Faith is at once a human decision and a divine gift. There are numerous Jewish parallels to this theological notion which will be discussed below.

The Similitudes of the Growing Seed and the Mustard Seed (vss. 26-32)

These similitudes are examples of the *parabolai* mentioned in vss. 11, 13, and 33-34, by which Jesus taught the people. They are related to the parable and the wisdom sayings in this collection by the motifs of the kingdom and the seed. Both are extended similes. It was said above, in Chapter 2, that a simile that is extended far enough hardly differs from an extended metaphor. As each of these similitudes develops, we become aware of two levels of meaning, so that the whole compositions may be said to be tropical. Literally, they have to do with the growth of seed; tropically, with the coming of the kingdom.

If proof is needed that an extended simile can be as obscure as an extended metaphor, surely the similitude of the growing seed provides it. It begins, "The kingdom of God is as if," yet it is notoriously difficult to interpret.[19] The scattering of the seed stands for the incipience of the kingdom, no doubt in the words and works of Jesus; the growth of the seed represents its development; and the putting in of the sickle at harvest time stands for the final judgment (as we know from Joel 3:13 and Apoc 14:14-20). Beyond that it is not possible to be more specific.

In the similitude of the mustard seed, the tiny seed stands for the humble beginning of the kingdom in the ministry of Jesus; its impressive growth as a shrub for its full development; and the birds which nest in its shade for the Gentile nations. The emphasis on the smallness of the seed and the largeness of the shrub makes it likely that the similitude is about the contrast between lowly beginnings and final splendid fulfillment. (For parallels to this similitude see Ezek 17:22-24; 31:1-18; Dan 4:10-27; 1 QH 8:4-36; it appears also in Gospel of Thomas 20. For the image of birds to represent the

---

19. Various interpretations of the similitude are summarized in A. E. J. Rawlinson, *St. Mark*, Westminster Commentaries (2nd ed.; London: Methuen, 1927) 55-56; Taylor, *St. Mark*, 265-66; and Dodd, *Parables*, 141-43.

Gentiles, see *1 Enoch* 90:30,33,37; *Midrash* to Ps 104:12 [LXX 103:12]. See also Jgs 9:15; Lam 4:20; Bar 1:12; Sir 14:26.)

Several observations need to be made. First, both similitudes speak of three stages: beginning, development, and full growth. If we reject the invalid principle that a similitude can have one "point" only, we need ignore none of these stages. What we have is a complete description of the coming of the kingdom. It begins inauspiciously in the ministry of Jesus; it attracts an increasing number of disciples; and finally it reaches its consummation.

Second, the similitudes illustrate well the paradox that the kingdom is at once present and future. Just as the full-grown harvest or shrub is in some way already contained in the small seed, but does not yet exist, so the kingdom is already breaking in with the words and works of Jesus, but has not yet come.[20]

Third, it should not be thought that these similitudes do not speak of growth, since they have to do with the kingdom, which was not understood by Jesus or the early Christians as a human society.[21] It must be said, against this, that the kingdom would have inhabitants, and that the final chosen people who would inhabit the kingdom was subject to growth. Jesus surely hoped for increasing numbers of those who would hear the word and repent, and thus become members of the people who would enter the kingdom when it came in fullness. Likewise the early Christians, including Mark, certainly understood the Church as the body of the elect who would inhabit the kingdom in the near future. The community of Jesus' followers, and later the community of Christians, thus constituted the vestibule of the kingdom. It is this growing eschatological community that the similitudes in part describe. Since the ancients probably did not make a neat conceptual distinction between the kingdom of God and the people who would inhabit the kingdom, they could speak of the growth of the eschatological community as though it were the growth of the kingdom itself.[22]

Fourth, it is therefore not correct to contrast too sharply the Markan version of the parable of the sower and the two similitudes on the grounds that the former speaks of the word, the latter of the kingdom. All three share the same subject. The kingdom must have inhabitants; those who will enter are those who have heard and kept the word; both the parable and the similitudes speak of the development of the community that will enter the kingdom—all three under the image of growing seed.

20. A notable exception to the widely held view that in these similitudes the beginning of growth corresponds to the activity of Jesus is, of course, Dodd, *Parables*, 143–44, 153–54, who says it is the gathering of the harvest and the full growth of the shrub that stand for Jesus' ministry, in which the kingdom has come.

21. As Bultmann, *Synoptic Tradition*, 200, says.

22. See the discussion of the view that eschatological and ecclesiological concerns do not cancel each other out in Karl Ludwig Schmidt, *The Church*, Bible Key Words (tr. J. R. Coates from *TWNT* II; London: Black, 1950) 41–42. Cf. Dahl, "Parables of Growth."

Conclusion: The Use of Parables (vss. 33–34)[23]

Verse 33 reminds us that only a few examples of Jesus' parables have been given here. Most commentators think that these two verses are contradictory, that vs. 33 describes Jesus' method of teaching by simple comparisons that could be understood by all, while vs. 34 restates the Markan theory of vss. 10–12. But the difficult expression, "as they were able to hear it," would seem to mean that the parables, though an indirect way of teaching, could be understood by those willing to make the necessary effort. This is not contradicted by what is said of Jesus giving explicit and direct explanations to the disciples. In vs. 11, in the private explanation of the parable of the sower, and in vs. 34, the disciples are depicted as the recipients and guardians of the teaching that was to come down to the Church. What could be comprehended by an attentive and meditative hearer was made explicit and unmistakably clear to the disciples.

B. SEMITIC PARALLELS TO THE MOTIFS IN MARK 4

Several motifs have been interwoven in this carefully worked-out chapter on the parables. It is worthwhile to isolate these motifs and to examine their parallels in the OT and Jewish literature. They are: (a) the parable as mysterious; (b) public pronouncement and private explanation; (c) *mystērion*; (d) hardness of heart; and (e) determinism and free will combined.

(a) *The parable as mysterious.* As has been pointed out in earlier chapters, a number of passages in the OT and Jewish literature refer to the parable as mysterious speech (Ezek 17:2; Hab 2:6; Ps 49:5 [LXX 48:5; RSV 49:4]; Ps 78:2 [LXX 77:2]; Prov 1:5b–6; Sir 39:2; 47:15 [LXX only]; 47:17 [Hebr only]; *1 Enoch* 68:1). It is out of the question, then, to say that Mark invented the idea. Rather, Mark stands at the end of a long Semitic tradition. It should be understood that the theory represents a sound insight on the part of the ancients, since the parable does in fact teach by indirect reference.

(b) *Public pronouncement and private explanation.* As Daube[24] has shown, the Markan account in which Jesus speaks a parable in public, then explains it to his disciples in private, is modeled on an established rabbinic type of narrative. In this narrative type, an opponent who asks a question of

---

23. On these verses see Willi Marxsen, "Redaktionsgeschichtliche Erklärung der sogenannten Parabeltheorie des Markus," *ZTK* 52 (1955) 255–71, esp. 262–63.

24. David Daube, "Public Pronouncement and Private Explanation in the Gospels," *ExpT* 57 (1945-46) 175–77; and David Daube, Ch. 6: "Public Retort and Private Explanation," *The New Testament and Rabbinic Judaism* (London: University of London, Athlone Press, 1956) 141–50. The same narrative type occurs at Mk 7:14–23; 10:2–12; and Mt 13:24–30,36–43. As Daube notes, in none of the rabbinic parallels is the rabbi's teaching a parable; it is always an interpretation of the Scriptures or the Law.

a rabbi is sent away with a misleading retort, then the rabbis' followers are given the real answer. Daube says of these narratives that they reflect a sharp division between those of the outside world, who do not deserve enlightenment, and the elect, who are entrusted with it. There is no justification, he insists, for mitigating the statement in Mk 4:10–12: the exclusion of "those outside" from understanding and salvation had always been an idea implicit in these rabbinic narratives.[25]

(c) *Mystērion*. The notion of divine mysteries is one which had a long history in pre-Christian Semitic thought. Brown[26] has examined the many references to "mystery" in the OT and Intertestamental literature. What follows here is taken largely from his thorough study.

Brown believes the concept had its origin in the *sôd*, the secret heavenly assembly of the deity and his council, which appears in the preexilic OT books. The Israelite prophet is one to whom is granted a vision of this heavenly assembly (see, e.g., Am 3:7), whose decisions concerning the world he then reveals to the people.

As is well known, the motif of divine secrets revealed to privileged persons occurs frequently in the postexilic books. Daniel 2 tells of a dream of King Nebuchadnezzar concerning the future of the Babylonian and succeeding kingdoms. The term "mystery" seems to refer both to the dream and to the things to come which it depicts (2:18–19,27–29,30,47). The dream and its interpretation are revealed to Daniel "in a vision of the night" (2:19), and this because he already possessed wisdom: for God "gives wisdom to the wise and knowledge to those who have understanding" (2:21).

Sirach, too, speaks of divine mysteries (*ta krypta* or *ta apokrypha*: 3:21–22; 11:4; 39:7; 42:19; 43:32; 48:24–25). Once these are cosmic mysteries or natural phenomena (43:32), twice they are secrets concerning what is to come in the future (42:19; 48:25). Wisdom is the agent of God who reveals mysteries (4:18; 14:21). One can learn these mysteries by studying the law, the writings, and the prophets (39:1), but also by meditating on the proverbs and parables of the scribes; these, as noted earlier, are regarded by Sirach as obscure sayings (39:2–3). There is a reference also to the "parables and riddles" (*parabolai ainigmatōn*) and "interpretations" (*hermēneiai*) of Solomon (47:15,17). There is no doubt that for Sirach proverbs and parables expressed divine mysteries.

The Wisdom of Solomon once speaks of God's plans for the afterlife of the just and the unjust as his "secret purposes" (*mystēria*: 2:22). One passage

---

25. Daube, "Public Retort," 142, 149. Daube does not, however, regard the Synoptic interpretation of the parables of the sower and the weeds among the wheat as authentic.

26. Brown, *Semitic Background of Term "Mystery."* See also J. Armitage Robinson, "On the meaning of *mystērion* in the New Testament," *St Paul's Epistle to the Ephesians* (London: Macmillan, 1903) 234–40; C. F. D. Moule, "Mystery," *IDB* III, 479–81; and Günther Bornkamm, "*mystērion, myeō*," *TDNT* IV, 802–828.

refers to the origin of Wisdom, its emanation from God, as a "secret" (*mystērion*: 6:22). Elsewhere, this work, composed in Greek, uses the term or related terms in a way that shows the influence of the Hellenistic mystery cult (7:21; 8:4; 12:5; 14:15,23).

The notion of mystery is developed further in the apocalyptic writings. In *1 Enoch*, there is mention of evil mysteries (e.g., 9:6-8; 16:3). The word refers also to natural phenomena or cosmic mysteries (41:3; ch. 52; 60:11; 71:4; 80:7). It refers frequently to the mysteries of God's will as it affects mankind, and to human actions (e.g., 63:3). The good and evil deeds of men are spoken of as mysteries which will be brought to light at the final judgment (38:3; 49:2,4; 61:9; 83:7; cf. Sir 1:30). The term "mystery" also refers to God's judgment, in particular to the mystery that the righteous shall be rewarded, but the evil punished (61:5; 68:5; 103:2). Finally, the term is applied to the judge himself, the Elect One or the Son of Man, who has been hidden, but who will be revealed on the last day to the elect (48:6-7; 62:1), when he "shall pour forth all the secrets of wisdom and counsel" (51:3; see also ch. 71). While for Sirach the mysteries could be learned by studying the Scriptures and the sayings of the scribes, here as in Daniel they are revealed in visions and explained by an angel to Enoch. As noted earlier, these visions are called parables (37:1; 38:1; 43:4; 45:1; 58:1; 60:1).

In *2 Esdras* there is only one type of mystery: the secrets concerning the destiny of Israel and the last times (10:38; 12:36-38; 14:5). The mysteries are revealed to the privileged Esdras in visions or speeches which are called parables (4:44-50; 8:1-3) and which are explained by the angel. These secrets are not to be given to everyone. Esdras is told that Moses had received a revelation on Sinai, and the Lord had commanded him: "These words you shall publish openly, and these you shall keep secret" (14:3-6). Likewise, only part of the written account of Esdras' vision (the twenty-four OT books) is to be given to his contemporaries in the Babylonian exile; the rest (seventy pseudepigraphical books) is to be given to "the wise" among his people who will preserve it for posterity (12:36-38; 14:26; 14:45-48). The notion of the hidden Son of Man appears again in *2 Esdras* (13:52).

In the Dead Sea Scrolls,[27] references to cosmic mysteries occur, especially in the Hymns (e.g., 1QH 1:11-13). As Vermes[28] has pointed out, throughout the Hymns the author thanks God for two things: for having been saved from the fate of the unrighteous, and for the gift of discernment of the divine mysteries. He acknowledges that no man has earned insight into these

---

27. For a list of occurrences of the term "mystery" in the Dead Sea Scrolls, see E. Vogt, "'Mysteria' in textibus Qumran," *Bib* 37 (1956) 247–57. See also W. D. Davies, "'Knowledge' in the Dead Sea Scrolls and Matthew 11:25-30," *HTR* 46 (1953) 113–39; and Lucien Cerfaux, "La connaissance des secrets du royaume d'après Mt., XIII,11 et parallèles," *Recueil L. Cerfaux* III (1962) 123–38.

28. Geza Vermes, *The Dead Sea Scrolls in English* (Baltimore: Penguin Books, 1962) 149.

mysteries; God graciously reveals them to the righteous (1:21; 7:26–32; 11:9–10; 12:11–20; 13:13–14). There occur also a few references to evil mysteries (1QS 14:9; 1QH 5:36).

The term "mystery" is often used to refer to God's plan for the unfolding of history. It is God's providence that controls the angels; by his mysteries, God allows the Angel of Darkness to lead the children of righteousness astray for a time (1QS 3:20–23), but he will destroy its domain at the end (1QS 4:18). Divine providence also affects the life of the individual man (1QM 16:11; 17:8–9; 1QH 9:23). Finally, it is God's providence that controls the ultimate destiny of Israel and the nations. The term "mystery" is used to refer to the final events (1QS 11:3–4). The most extensive use of "mystery" in an apocalyptic sense is that in the Commentary on Habakkuk 2:1–4a, where it is said that not even the prophets knew "when time would come to an end" (1QpHab 7:1–7).

The term "mystery" is also used to refer to the Qumran community's special interpretation of the law. The Damascus Rule recounts how, beginning with the wandering in the wilderness, there occurred a process of historical selection, until the faithful remnant was narrowed down to the Qumran community, which thus became the guardian of commandments hidden from the rest of Israel. What are these hidden commands? They are such things as God's "holy Sabbaths and His glorious feasts, the testimonies of His righteousness and the ways of His truth, and the desires of His will which a man must do in order to live" (CD 3:12–20; cf. 1QS 11:5–8). The writer of the Hymns seems to have played a special role in interpreting these mysteries and instructing others in them (1QH 2:13–14; 4:27–28).

A point important to note is that these mysteries of the law were revealed only to the sectarians, who were strictly forbidden to disclose them to outsiders (1QH 5:25–26; 1QS 4:6; 9:17–22). One passage shows, however, that the outsiders themselves were responsible for their exclusion, for they had willfully refused to understand the mysteries: "They have neither inquired nor sought after Him concerning His laws that they might know the hidden things in which they have sinfully erred; and matters revealed they have treated with insolence" (1QS 5:11).

An important passage concerning the community's authentic interpretation of the law is the allegory of the tree (1QH 8:4–36). According to Brown, the allegory is to be understood as follows: God set a plantation of trees (the elect among the Israelites) beside "a mysterious fountain" (the correct interpretation of the law). The trees "put out a shoot of the everlasting Plant" (the Qumran community) which was persecuted by the other trees. "And the bud of the shoot of holiness for the Plant of truth was hidden and was not esteemed; and being unperceived, its mystery was sealed" (possibly a reference to the Teacher of Righteousness). It is said that "No [man shall approach] the well-spring of life . . . who seeing has not discerned, and considering has not believed in the fountain of life." The allegory ends with the ultimate victory of the community.[29]

The numerous parallels to the Markan treatment of the concept of *mysterion* are readily apparent, and need not be belabored here. Mark has obviously taken over several different aspects of the Semitic notion.

(d) *Hardness of heart.*[30] The expression "hardness of heart" does not occur at Mk 4:10–12 (although it appears in the quotation of the same passage from Isaiah at Jn 12:40). It does, however, appear elsewhere in Mark. Twice Jesus accuses the Pharisees of hardness of heart (Mk 3:5; 10:5). Twice the charge is leveled at the disciples after the miracles of the loaves, both times precisely for their failure to understand the miracles (Mk 6:52; 8:17). Though the expression is absent, the concept of hardness of heart is very much present in Mk 4:10–12.

This concept, too, had a long history in the Israelite tradition. Yahweh several times hardens the heart of Pharaoh (e.g., at Ex 4:21; 7:3; 10:20; 14:4); he does the same to Sihon king of Heshbon (Dt 2:30). These are non-Israelites; but the Israelites too are often called "hard of heart" (Isa 46:12; Lam 3:65; Ezek 2:4–5,7). And there are other examples of Israel's hardness of heart where the term does not appear: the Israelites failed to believe that God would lead them into Canaan (Num 13–14); Ahaz refused to rely on Yahweh during the Syro-Ephraimitic crisis (Isa 7:1–8:15).

It is most interesting to note that in several of these passages hardness of heart is the refusal to see, to hear, or to understand the word of God (Isa 6:9–10; Ezek 2:4–5,7; 3:7). Elsewhere, too, we read of Israelites who have eyes but will not see, and ears but will not hear (Dt 29:2–4; Jer 5:21; Ezek 3:27; 12:2). Hardness of heart, blindness, and deafness are three equivalent terms for obduracy; their opposites are faith and repentance.[31]

(e) *Determinism and free will combined.* The predominant OT view of morality is, of course, that man bears the responsibility for his actions, good and evil. Nevertheless, there also appears throughout the OT a doctrine of determinism. God says to Abimelech, "it was I who kept you from sinning against me" (Gen 20:6). As noted above, it is the Lord who many times

29. Brown, *Semitic Background of Term "Mystery,"* 26–27.

30. See J. Armitage Robinson, "On *pōrōsis* and *pērōsis*," *St Paul's Epistle to the Ephesians* (London: Macmillan, 1903) 264–74; Friedrich Baumgärtel and Johannes Behm, "*kardia, kardiognōstēs, sklērokardia*," TDNT III, 605–614; and Karl Ludwig Schmidt and Martin Anton Schmidt, "*pachynō, pōroō (pēroō), pōrōsis (pērōsis), sklēros, sklērotēs, sklērotrachēlos, sklērynō*," *TDNT* V, 1022–31.

31. Discussions of the theological problem of hardness of heart are found in Lucien Cerfaux, "'L'aveuglement d'esprit' dans l'Evangile de Saint Marc," *Le Muséon* (Mélanges L. Th. Lefort) 59 (1946) 267–79; Krister Stendahl, "The Called and the Chosen. An Essay on Election," in *The Root of the Vine: Essays in Biblical Theology* (ed. A. G. Hebert; New York: Philosophical Library, 1953) 63–80; and Frank E. Eakin Jr., "Spiritual Obduracy and Parable Purpose," in *The Use of the Old Testament in the New and Other Essays: Studies in Honor of William Franklin Stinespring* (ed. James M. Efird; Durham, N.C.: Duke University Press, 1972) 87–109.

hardens the heart of Pharaoh, and so controls the historical events surrounding the Exodus. He puts "a lying spirit in the mouth" of Ahab's
prophets in order to deceive the king (1 Kgs 22:21-23). It is the Lord who
commands Isaiah to make the people obdurate (Isa 6:9-10) in the passage
quoted in Mk 4:12. Later in Isaiah the Israelites complain to God, "why dost
thou make us err from thy ways and harden our heart, so that we fear thee
not?" (Isa 63:17); and "thou wast angry, and we sinned" (Isa 64:4; RSV
64:5).

Russell[32] speaks of the combination of determinism and free will in
apocalypticism. He writes that the conflict between human freedom and
divine control had not yet emerged as a problem, and that the two ideas
could be expressed side by side without any noticeable difficulty.[33] The two
views often appear together in the same work (*Jub.* 5:13 and 41:24; *2 Enoch*
53:2 and 30:15; *Ps. Sol.* 14:5 and 9:7; *2 Apoc. Bar.* 48:40; 85:7). Not only a
man's life, but his afterlife, is predetermined (*1 Enoch* 41:8; *2 Enoch* 49:2; *2
Apoc. Bar.* 42:7; *Ps. Sol.* 5:6); yet his state in the afterlife will depend on the
choices he has freely made (*Jub.* 21:25; 22:10; *1 Enoch* 41:1; 43:2; 61:8; *2
Apoc. Bar.* 14:12; 54:15,19).

Brown[34] has noted the same juxtaposition in the Qumran literature, the
result, he believes, of the combination of OT ideas of morality, reward and
punishment, with the Zoroastrian notion of two spirits, the spirits of truth
and falsehood, with man under the dominion of one or the other. A number
of passages which speak of the two spirits are deterministic (1QS 3:15;
4:15,24; CD 7:19). Moreover, it is said that the sons of light have been
chosen by a gracious act of God (1QS 4:22; 8:6; 11:7; 1QH 1). Other
passages, however, assert a doctrine of free will (virtuous works are
emphasized throughout 1QS, as is repentance, and even members of the
community are blamed for their evil acts). Wicked deeds are committed by
free choice (1QS 3:1; 5:11; CD 3:7; 4:9-10). The sectarians, Brown observes,
never discussed the conflict between these two notions, or attempted a
speculative solution.[35]

Lauterbach[36] points out the same combination in the rabbinic literature,
which offers perhaps the closest parallels to the Markan passage. As
Josephus accurately reported (*War* 2.8.14; *Antiq.* 13.5.9; 18.1.3), the Phari-

32. David Syme Russell, *The Method and Message of Jewish Apocalyptic, 200 BC-AD 100*
(Philadelphia: Westminster, 1964) 230-34.

33. Russell, *Jewish Apocalyptic*, 232.

34. Raymond E. Brown, Ch. 7: "The Qumran Scrolls and the Johannine Gospel and
Epistles," *New Testament Essays* (Milwaukee, Wis.: Bruce, 1965) 102-131, esp. 112-16. (A
reprint of the article in *CBQ* 17 [1955] 403-419, 559-74; and in *The Scrolls and the New
Testament* [ed. Krister Stendahl; New York: Harper, 1957] 183-207.)

35. Brown, "Qumran Scrolls," *NT Essays*, 112-13.

36. Jacob Z. Lauterbach, *The Pharisees and Their Teachings* (New York: Bloch, 1930)
61-62.

sees joined the doctrines of divine providence and free will. "Everything is in the hands of God but the fear of God" (*b. Ber* 33b), they held; "Everything is foreseen, yet freedom of choice is given" (*Pirqe Aboth* 3:15). Despite their belief in free will, says Lauterbach, they could not deny God the power to determine man's choices if they were to uphold the doctrine of his omnipotence. Besides, he notes, they knew the OT passages where God controlled men's actions.[37]

How, then, did they reconcile the two? Lauterbach gives this clear answer: they concluded that God can, but does not will to, determine man's conduct; man is left to decide for himself. However, God is prepared to assist man when he chooses to do good, and to refrain from impeding him when he chooses to do evil, thus in a sense cooperating with him.[38] He cites in this connection the Talmudic sayings: "If a man chooses to do good the heavenly powers help him. If he chooses to do evil, they leave the way open to him" (*b. Shabb* 104a); and "In whatever way man desires to go the heavenly powers lead him" (*b. Mak* 10b).

What we have here is nothing other than the doctrine expressed in Mk 4:24–25.[39] Rabbinic parallels to the saying, "the measure you give will be the measure you get" (vs. 24a) occur (*Mekilta* 13:19; *Sotah* 1:7; *Siphre* on Num 12:14). More important yet are the parallels to the further idea, "and still more will be given you. For to him who has will more be given; and from him who has not, even what he has will be taken away" (vss. 24b–25). This is the doctrine "that God helps the good to become better and the bad worse" (*Mekilta* on Ex 19:5; 15:26; *Siphre* on Num 9:8; 15:36; 27:5; *b. Ber* 40a; 55a; *b. B B* 12b).[40]

What is most interesting is that this bit of moral theology appears in the rabbinic documents linked to the idea of hearing and understanding. Two passages are worth quoting:

A mortal can put something into an empty vessel but not into a full one. But the Holy One, blessed be He, is not so; He puts more into a full vessel but not into an empty one; for it says, *If hearkening thou wilt hearken* [Ex 15:26], implying, if thou hearkenest [once] thou wilt go on hearkening, and if not, thou wilt not hearken.

(*b. Ber* 40a)

R. Johanan said: The Holy One, blessed be He, gives wisdom only to one who already has wisdom, as it says, *He giveth wisdom unto the wise, and knowledge to them that know understanding* [Dan 2:21]. R. Taḥlifa from the West [Palestine] heard and repeated it before R. Abbahu. He said to him: You learn it from there, but we learn it

---

37. Lauterbach, *Pharisees*, 61.

38. Lauterbach, *Pharisees*, 61–62.

39. Rabbinic parallels to Mk 4:21–25 are discussed by Morton Smith, *Tannaitic Parallels to the Gospels*, JBL Monograph Series, VI (1951; corrected reprint, 1968) 135–37.

40. Smith, *Tannaitic Parallels*, 136.

from this text, namely, *In the hearts of all that are wise-hearted I have put wisdom* [Ex 31:6; i.e., the Pentateuch is superior].

(*b. Ber* 55a)[41]

Lauterbach observes, in much the same vein as Russell and Brown, that the Pharisees were not philosophers and apparently did not realize all the ramifications and problems of their simple solution.[42]

To conclude: the Semitic parallels to the principal motifs which appear in Mark 4 show that the Markan parable theory stays well within Jewish categories. There is in fact nothing in the parable chapter which is not derived from Palestinian Jewish theology of the first century. The Markan theory is quite in harmony with its religio-historical background.

---

41. The translations are from *The Babylonian Talmud* (ed. Isadore Epstein; 34 vols.; London: Soncino Press, 1935-48), *Berakoth* (tr. Maurice Simon).

42. Lauterbach, *Pharisees*, 62.

5

THE MARKAN THEME OF MYSTERY

Other Markan passages are related to the parable discourse (4:1–34) by a common motif, the incomprehension of the audience, especially the disciples: these are the wisdom saying which occurs in the discussion on what defiles (7:14–23); and the two miracles of the loaves, each of which is followed by an incident on the water (6:30–52; 8:1–21).[1] The present chapter has a twofold purpose: to show how such diverse things as parable, wisdom saying, and miracle story can be brought into relation in Mark's Gospel; and to shed some light on the theme of mysteriousness which unifies these passages and the entire Gospel. This final chapter first examines the wisdom saying and miracles, then states the general conclusions which follow from the present investigation concerning the Markan theme of the mystery of the kingdom.

A. THE WISDOM SAYING ON WHAT DEFILES (7:14–23)[2]

The topic of Mark 7, one of the most important chapters in the Gospel, is ceremonial purity *vs.* purity of heart. In this chapter, during a lively exchange with the Pharisees, scribes, and people on the subject of cleanness, Jesus declares null and void the laws of cultic purity of the Jewish religion (vss. 1–23)—once again quoting Isaiah (29:13, following the LXX). This astonishing teaching marks a turning-point in the ministry of Jesus; it brings to a close his work in Galilee and precedes his journey into the Gentile region of Tyre and Sidon (vs. 24).

Jesus has been debating the questions of the washing of hands and the Corban with the Pharisees and scribes alone, pointing out that what matters is not outward but inward cleanness, not the commandments of men but the commandment of God (vss. 1–13). He now calls the people to him, and pronounces a saying publicly. This is in keeping with Mk 4:34a: "he did not

---

1. The Markan similitudes of the fig tree (13:28–29) and the returning householder (13:33–37) and the parable of the wicked tenants (12:1–12) are omitted from the present discussion only because the concern of this chapter is with the theme of misunderstanding or mystery, which does not figure *directly* in these passages.

2. The wisdom saying appears in a simpler version in the Gospel of Thomas 14. For discussions of the Markan saying see the commentaries on the Gospel of Mark listed in the bibliography. An excellent treatment is that of Claude Goldsmid Montefiore, *The Synoptic Gospels*: I. *Introduction and Gospel of Mark* (2nd ed.; New York: KTAV Publishing House, 1968) 152–66.

speak to them without a parable"—for Mark refers to this saying as a *parabolē* (vs. 17). The prefatory words, "Hear me, all of you, and understand" (vs. 14), like the introduction to the parable of the sower, are a solemn call to attentive hearing. They carry the suggestion of great authority in the speaker; and they warn that the words to follow are both important and indirect. The saying itself is the climax of the chapter. Though momentous, it is brief: "there is nothing outside a man which by going into him can defile him; / but the things which come out of a man are what defile him" (vs. 15).[3]

The pronouncement is not, strictly speaking, a parable. It is a wisdom saying composed of two lines which are antithetically parallel. The antithesis consists both of the use of opposites (what goes into a man, what comes out of a man), and of negative and positive assertions (does not defile, does defile). Thus we have the structure:

What goes into a man   /   does not defile;
What comes out of a man   /   does defile.[4]

As observed earlier, the framework of the saying is periphrasis or circumlocution, which is not a trope. (See above, Chapter 2, Section C.) Yet implied in this saying are two levels of meaning. The words in the first line, "nothing outside a man which by going into him," are circumlocution for food. But the corresponding words in the second line, "the things which come out of a man," can be circumlocution for two things: bodily waste matter, and immorality.[5] The periphrasis, that is, has within it something like an *implicit* metaphor, in which the body's unclean discharges stand for the person's immoral thoughts, words, and deeds. On one level the saying states the obvious fact that it is not food, but excrement, that defiles physically; on another level it teaches that it is not food, but evil thoughts, words, and deeds, that defile religiously. The implied trope changes the antithesis in the two lines from a contrast between material and material thing (food *vs.* bodily waste) to a contrast between material and spiritual thing (food *vs.* immorality). The saying is thus an exceptionally well constructed one, and the shift from the material to the spiritual reference in its two lines, far from being a flaw (as is sometimes said), is an intended and brilliant play or turn (*tropos*) on meaning.

---

3. The manuscript evidence suggests that the conclusion in vs. 16, "If any man has ears to hear, let him hear," is a later addition. According to *The Greek New Testament*, ed. Kurt Aland *et al.*, the following omit the verse: א B L Δ* etc.; the following include it: A D K W X Δ^c θ Π etc.

4. The structure of the wisdom saying is analyzed by Burney, *Poetry of Our Lord*, 71–74.

5. The possible reference to bodily waste is noted in the commentaries of John Bowman, *The Gospel of Mark: The New Christian Jewish Passover Haggadah, SPB* 8 (Leiden: Brill, 1965) 168–69; A. Loisy, *L'Evangile selon Marc* (Paris: Émile Nourry, 1912) 210. Montefiore, *Mark*, 162, mentions leprosy, eruptions, and so on.

Since what we have here is a wisdom saying and not strictly speaking a parable, it may be asked in what sense Mark could speak of it as a *parabolē*. It will be recalled that for the ancients, both Israelite and Greek, the term *māšāl* or *parabolē* could be used of *any* speech that was out of the ordinary or in some way striking; in Israel it seems to have been used especially of obscure speech. In antiquity, as noted, the term was not restricted to the narrower class which is called "parable" in modern scholarship. (See Chapter 2, Section A; and Appendix.) This utterance could, then, be called a *parabolē* by Mark on more than one account. First, as a wisdom saying, with its carefully wrought antithetic parallelism, it is not ordinary or everyday, but extraordinary and impressive speech. Second, it is speech that is not easy to understand, and this for two reasons. For one thing, periphrasis is reference to a thing in a roundabout and indirect way; the hearer must be attentive and perspicacious if he is to know what the thing is which is being referred to. For another, the metaphor implicit within this particular periphrasis gives to the saying two levels of meaning—and, again, the hearer might fail to arrive at the indirect but more important level. Thus a saying like this one could function much like a parable.

Because they have not understood, the disciples, alone with Jesus, ask him about the saying (vs. 17), which he then expounds for them (vss. 18–23). This is in keeping with Mk 4:34b: "but privately to his own disciples he explained everything." Yet Jesus rebukes them: "Then are you also without understanding?" (vs. 18a), thus implying that, after all, they could and should have understood. If the historical context of the saying (assuming its authenticity) was in fact a discussion of outward and inward purity, then that would have provided the clue to its meaning, and Mark in this case would be correct in indicating that it could be comprehended by one who was willing to hear. Without such a context, however, its meaning would be more difficult to discern.

As the interpretation makes unequivocally clear, by this saying Jesus "declared all foods clean" (vs. 19b). In the preceding discussion concerning the washing of hands and the Corban, Jesus had effectively disposed of the oral law, the traditions of the scribes and Pharisees, characterizing them as laws of men which were not only inferior but at times even inimical to the law of God. Now, however, it is the written law itself which he puts aside, nullifying as he does the dietary laws of Leviticus (11–15) and Deuteronomy (14)—which his audience could only understand as that law of God to which he had earlier appealed! The teaching here thus portrays the consummate authority of Jesus, who stands above even the Mosaic commandments.

This saying is perhaps unequaled in importance for Christian moral theology. It has been remarked that it seems to sum up the ethics of Christianity and to set it over against the ethics of Judaism.[6] To abrogate the

---

6. Branscomb, *Mark*, 125.

food laws written in the very Scriptures is a bold enough stroke in itself; but the saying does even more. As Montefiore[7] has said, its principle goes far beyond its wording: the saying annuls the whole concept of material or cultic impurity (which regards uncleanness as unholiness) held by so many religions of antiquity, including Judaism. This remarkably original saying, then, represents a great step forward in the history of religion. It removes uncleanness, or unholiness, from the realm of material things and situates it exclusively in the realm of ethics, thus fixing the responsibility for it on the person himself.[8]

The saying places Jesus in the tradition of the great prophets, who excoriated a mere external fulfillment of ceremonial commandments (Isa 1:11–17; 58; Jer 7:21–26; Hos 6:6; Am 5:21–27; Ps 51:20–21 [LXX 50:20–21; RSV 51:18–19]). But the pronouncement is more than a prophetic saying. If the Israelite prophets had urged, not that cultic religious practices be eliminated, but that they be informed by social justice, the Markan saying goes much further along the same line of thought. It recalls the words of Jesus earlier in Mark: "No one sews a piece of unshrunk cloth on an old garment," and "no one puts new wine into old wineskins" (2:21–22). We have here not merely a reform of the old, but a replacement of the old by the new. Only the agent ushering in the kingdom could bring with him such daring change.

It becomes clear why the saying is presented as mysterious, theologically speaking, in the Gospel of Mark. Once again, it is not intellectual inability but moral unwillingness that prevents the hearers from grasping the import of the pronouncement. All of their religious heritage, written and oral, had taught them that the divine law itself distinguished between clean and unclean foods and other things material; hence their resistance to the revolutionary teaching they now heard. In this saying, they were shown nothing less than the sharp break between the old age and the new, between the law and the prophets and the kingdom of God. Having eyes, they would not see. Confronted with a choice, they proved unwilling to forgo their traditions. As Cranfield[9] has said, the key to the mystery is that Jesus here speaks as the *telos nomou* (Rom 10:4), the one to whom the law and the prophets bear witness and in whom they are fulfilled; the mystery is none other than the mystery of the kingdom, breaking in with the ministry of Jesus.

The arguments concerning the genuineness of the saying and its interpretation, extensively presented elsewhere, need not be rehearsed here.[10] It

---

7. Montefiore, *Mark*, 153.
8. Bowman, *Mark*, 169.
9. Cranfield, *Saint Mark*, 244–45.
10. See Branscomb, *Mark*, 125–27; Cranfield, *Saint Mark*, 240, 242–43; Montefiore, *Mark*, 163; Nineham, *St Mark*, 191–93; Taylor, *St. Mark*, 342–43, 346–47.

might simply be mentioned that the saying, if genuine, could well have meant on the lips of Jesus what similar pronouncements meant on the lips of an Isaiah or an Amos: not that cultic-ritual laws are utterly unimportant, but only that they are less important than moral laws. If this was the case, it would explain how the Church, for example at Jerusalem and Antioch, would later need to engage in debate on the question of the continued validity of the Jewish commandments. It would explain, too, in what sense the saying was taken as mysterious in Mark's time: the full implication of the pronouncement—that it calls for the abolishment of all food laws—was not seen by the first audience and only gradually came to light. Mark (or someone before him) could, by using the device of public pronouncement and private explanation, again portray the inner circle of disciples as the bearers of authentic tradition. He could also, by interpreting the saying in its fullest sense, employ it to give the authority of Jesus to the Hellenistic Church's break from Judaism.

The pericope which immediately follows is closely related to the section on ceremonial purity *vs.* purity of heart. Having gone into the region of Tyre and Sidon, Jesus heals the daughter of the Syrophoenician woman, thus signaling his change of orientation away from the Jewish and toward the Gentile world (7:24–30). In this miracle, Jesus grants to the Syrophoenician mother and daughter the saving help that up to that time had been reserved for the children of Israel. The metaphor for such blessings, it is interesting to observe, is "bread" (vs. 27); possibly we have in the word an association between this and the miracles of the loaves which precede (6:32–44) and follow it (8:1–10), and perhaps also to the previous discussion of food laws (7:14–23). It has been observed that the wisdom saying on what defiles and the miracle of the Syrophoenician woman together are equivalent to Acts 10:1–11:18, which narrate the vision to Peter revealing that no animal is unclean and his subsequent preaching of the gospel to Cornelius the Roman centurion.[11]

The following miracle, the healing of the deaf-mute (7:31–37), which occurs evidently in the Gentile district of the Decapolis, is probably to be understood eschatologically. Verse 37 appears to interpret the miracle as a fulfillment of the prophecy in Isa 35:5–6a regarding the end-time: "Then the eyes of the blind shall be opened, and the ears of the deaf unstopped; then shall the lame man leap like a hart, and the tongue of the dumb sing for joy."[12] The miracle may also be intended to illustrate the theological theme of hearing the word.

11. Montefiore, *Mark*, 163 (quoting B. W. Bacon, *The Gospel of Mark*, 147).

12. As Nineham, *St Mark*, 202, points out, the Markan adjective *mogilalos* (vs. 32), literally "having difficulty in speaking," is a rare Greek word which appears in only one other place in the Greek Bible, Isa 35:6.

B. THE TWO MIRACLES OF THE LOAVES AND INCIDENTS ON THE SEA (6:30–52; 8:1–21)

Mark intends that the two feeding miracles, each of which is followed by an incident on the lake (6:30–52 and 8:1–21), be understood as in some way similar to the parables. This intention is indicated by the conclusions to the two episodes. The first ends: "for they [the disciples] did not understand about the loaves, but their hearts were hardened" (6:52); the second closes with Jesus' rebuke to the disciples concerning the loaves: "Do you not yet perceive or understand? Are your hearts hardened? Having eyes do you not see, and having ears do you not hear? And do you not remember?" and again, "Do you not yet understand?" (8:17b–18,21). The present section will address the question raised by these verses as to how precisely miracles are like parables in Mark's Gospel.

Mk 6:30–52

The feeding of the five thousand (6:30–44) is followed immediately by Jesus' walking on the water (6:45–52). That the feeding miracle has about it some meaning which the disciples should have apprehended is clear, since it is expressly stated in the verse just quoted (6:52) which brings this pair of narratives to a close. The question is, what is the meaning, or revelation, conveyed by the miracle which disciple and reader alike, were they not hard of heart, would perceive? A variety of answers have been advanced; these are here summarized, and then an interpretation of the pair of miracles, at the redaction-critical level, is proposed.

The passage apparently makes several allusions to the OT. As a preface to the feeding, Mark says that Jesus had compassion on the crowd, for "they were like sheep without a shepherd" (vs. 34a). The simile is a borrowing from the LXX (Num 27:17; 1 Kgs 22:17; 2 Chr 18:16; Ezek 34:5; Jdt 11:19; cf. Isa 40:11; Jer 31:10; Zech 13:7; 2 Apoc. Bar. 2:52; Mk 14:27). Mark then reports that Jesus "began to teach them many things" (vs. 34b), characteristically without specifying what he taught.

It has been suggested by not a few commentators[13] that the feeding of the crowd in a desert place recalls the feeding of the Israelites in the wilderness (Ex 16; Num 11; for the Israelites' remembrance of the miracle see Neh 9:15; Pss 78:17–32 [LXX 77:17–32]—note the motif of obduracy here; 105:40 [LXX 104:40]). The two events are essentially the same: the miraculous provision of nourishment for a large number of people in a desert setting.

---

13. E.g., Bowman, *Mark*, 156–59; Cranfield, *Saint Mark*, 222; Sherman E. Johnson, *A Commentary on the Gospel According to St. Mark*, Black's New Testament Commentaries (London: Black, 1960) 122; Nineham, *St Mark*, 178.

The Markan term for "a lonely place" (erēmos topos, vss. 31,32,35) echoes the LXX word for "wilderness" in the Exodus narrative (erēmos, Ex 16:1,3,10,14,32). The incredulous question, how so many could be fed with so few resources (vs. 37), is a resonance of the similar question in the Numbers account (Num 11:21–22). Possibly the orderly seating of the crowd is based on the orderly arrangement of the Israelites during the wandering (Ex 18:13–27). If the Exodus event lies in the background, Mark's reference to "the green grass" (vs. 39) may be intended to indicate the Passover season.[14]

It has also been frequently proposed[15] that the Markan narrative is patterned on the miracle story of Elisha, in which the prophet fed a hundred men with a mere twenty barley loaves and some ears of grain (2 Kgs 4:42–44; cf. 1 Kgs 17:8–16; 2 Kgs 4:1–7). Elisha's command to give the men something to eat is similar to that of Jesus (1 Kgs 4:42b; Mk 6:37a); and both stories conclude with the astonishing statement that all present ate and still they had some left (1 Kgs 4:43b,44b; Mk 6:42–43). The Elisha stories, it has been noted,[16] may themselves have been influenced by the Exodus narrative.

That the miraculous feeding seems to point not only back to OT events, but also forward to the Last Supper and institution of the eucharist has often been observed.[17] Cranfield[18] has shown the similarity between the two moments in Jesus' ministry by setting the Markan passages (6:40ff. and 14:22ff.; cf. 1 Cor 11:23–24) in parallel columns. The identity of Jesus' actions in 6:41 and 14:22, in particular, suggests that Mark deliberately designed the parallelism. A few interpreters[19] have also seen in the distribution of the bread by the disciples a reference to the later distribution of the eucharist by the deacons at the Lord's Supper.

The explicit elaboration of both the manna and the eucharistic themes in the Johannine account of the feeding (Jn 6:30–34,48–51) supports the view that such an interpretation of the miracle could have existed in the tradition

14. So Ezra Palmer Gould, *A Critical and Exegetical Commentary According to St. Mark*, International Critical Commentary (New York: Scribner's, 1896) 118; M.-J. Lagrange, *Evangile selon Saint Marc*, Etudes bibliques (4th ed.; Paris: Librairie Lecoffre, 1947) 169; Josef Schmid, *The Gospel According to Mark*, The Regensburg New Testament (tr. and ed. Kevin Condon from 5th German ed.; Staten Island, N.Y.: Alba House, 1969) 129; Swete, *St Mark*, 133.

15. E.g., by Bowman, *Mark*, 155; Cranfield, *Saint Mark*, 222; Johnson, *St. Mark*, 122, 124; Montefiore, *Mark*, 125; Nineham, *St Mark*, 178.

16. Paul J. Achtemeier, "The Origin and Function of the Pre-Marcan Miracle Catenae," *JBL* 91 (1972) 204.

17. See, e.g., Cranfield, *Saint Mark*, 222–23; Hunter, *Saint Mark*, 73; Johnson, *St. Mark*, 121–22; Lagrange, *Saint Marc*, 171; Alfred Loisy, *Les évangiles synoptiques*, I (Paris: Ceffonds, 1907) 936–37; and *Marc*, 191, 194–96; Montefiore, *Mark*, 125; Nineham, *St Mark*, 177, 179; Taylor, *St. Mark*, 321, 324.

18. Cranfield, *Saint Mark*, 222.

19. Johnson, *St. Mark*, 125; Rawlinson, *St Mark*, 87.

as early as Mark's time. Indeed Paul, even before Mark, had connected the eucharist with the "supernatural food" of the Israelites in the wilderness (1 Cor 10:3ff.). That these related motifs were an intended part of the meaning of the Markan narrative cannot then be regarded as improbable.

Another suggestion, first made by Schweitzer[20] and often restated by others,[21] is that the miraculous feeding as recounted by Mark is an anticipation of the messianic banquet. According to Schweitzer, the feeding of the multitude is more than a foretaste of the banquet; it is a guarantee to those present that they will take part also in the messianic feast. The meal is thus, to use the felicitous expression of Schweitzer, an eschatological sacrament. The same is true of the Last Supper, as is shown by Jesus' reference there to the future drinking of the wine in the kingdom (Mk 14:25).

Some interpret the bread as a metaphor for the gift of revelation conveyed in the preaching of Jesus (referred to in 6:34b), and take the miracle story as a demonstration of his authority to teach.[22] Others interpret the feeding as a symbol for spiritual gifts (cf. 1 Cor 3:2; 1 Pet 2:2),[23] understanding the bread as a metaphor for both word and sacrament, or for Jesus as bread of life.[24] Other exegetes point out the homiletic purpose of the story, reading it as an assurance to Christians that the Lord will provide heavenly food, the eucharist, in the desert of this world.[25]

The miracle of the walking on water (6:45–52) is generally regarded as an epiphany, manifesting in some way Jesus' being and status. It seems intended to pose again a question like that at 4:41: "Who then is this, that even wind and sea obey him?" The answer is that he is Lord of the elements. Thus far exegetes are largely in agreement; there is less consensus on more specific questions as to what biblical motifs, if any, are at work in this portrayal of Jesus' person.

One suggestion[26] is that the narrative draws on those OT and Intertestamental passages where God is described as alone having power to walk over or through the water (Job 9:8; Ps 77:20 [LXX 76:20; RSV 77:19]; Isa 43:16;

---

20. Albert Schweitzer, *The Mystery of the Kingdom of God* (tr. Walter Lowrie; New York: Schocken Books, 1964 [German ed., 1901]) 168–74; and *The Quest of the Historical Jesus* (tr. W. Montgomery from 1st German ed. [1906]; New York: Macmillan, 1961) 376–82.

The idea of the messianic banquet appears in Isa 55:1ff.; cf. Isa 25:6ff. and 65:13ff.; *1 Enoch* 24–25; 62:14; 1QSa II; and in Mt 8:11 = Lk 13:29; Lk 14:15; Mk 14:25 = Mt 26:29 = Lk 22:18; Lk 22:16,30; cf. Apoc 2:17; 7:16–17, where the shepherd and feeding motifs occur together; 19:9.

21. Cranfield, *Saint Mark*, 223; Hunter, *Saint Mark*, 73; Johnson, *St. Mark*, 122; Nineham, *St Mark*, 178–79; Taylor, St. Mark, 321, 324–25.

22. E.g., Eduard Schweizer, *The Good News According to Mark*, Das Neue Testament Deutsch (tr. Donald H. Madvig; Richmond, Va.: John Knox, 1970) 138–40.

23. Johnson, *St. Mark*, 122.

24. Cranfield, *Saint Mark*, 223; Loisy, *Evangiles*, I, 936–38; and *Marc*, 193–96.

25. Nineham, *St Mark*, 179; Rawlinson, *St Mark*, 85.

26. Cranfield, *Saint Mark*, 229; Lagrange, *Saint Marc*, 173; Loisy, *Evangiles*, I, 942, n. 3; Taylor, *St. Mark*, 329.

Ps. Sol. 39; cf. Job 38:16; Sir 24:5).[27] It is worth noting that the verse in Second Isaiah refers to the Israelites' passing through the Red Sea (Ex 14–15) and that the prophet is here predicting a new and greater Exodus. If such OT passages as these constitute the background, then Jesus is here depicted as more than a wonder-worker, more than the Messiah of Judaism, but as Son of God.[28]

Dibelius[29] says the story may have to do with the "mythical waters of death"; and Bultmann[30] suggests it may be a displaced resurrection story. In differing ways, both Loisy[31] and Lohmeyer[32] arrive at an interpretation of the sea miracle as a victory over death. For Lohmeyer, the clue lies in the symbolism of water, which in the OT and Jewish literature is a recurrent metaphor for suffering, fear, and death (2 Sam 22:5; Pss 18:16; 46:1–3 [LXX 17:17; 45:2–4]; *Ps. Sol.* 39; see n. 27 above). In the feeding miracle Jesus is presented as Lord of life, in the sea miracle as conqueror of death. In the second miracle the disciples are saved from wind and sea; on Lohmeyer's interpretation, they are rescued from death, and we have a perfect explanation for what would otherwise appear to be the combination of two originally separate stories, a calming of a storm and an epiphany.

For Loisy, this miracle is a pointer to the supreme miracle of Jesus' resurrection. The clue lies in the disciples' terror at seeing a figure they take

27. Following are other references to the waters cited by Nineham, *Mark*, 146: the divine powers over the sea (Pss 89:8–10; 93:3–4; 106:8–9 [LXX 88:9–11; 92:3–4; 105:8–9]; Isa 51:10); the use of storm as a metaphor for evil forces (Pss 69:1–2,14–15; 18:16 [LXX 68:2–3,15–16; 17:17], etc,); and the confidence which men ought to have in God even in the midst of the greatest disturbance (Pss 46:1–3; 65:7; 107:23–32 [LXX 45:2–4; 64:8; 106:23–32]; Isa 43:2).

28. So Schmid, *Mark*, 132.

The words by which Jesus identifies himself, *egō eimi* (vs. 50b), are ordinary Greek for "it is I." Nevertheless, they may allude to the same words of Yahweh in the OT (Ex 3:14, a theophany; Dt 32:39; Isa 43:10; 52:6). This suggestion is made by Cranfield, *Saint Mark*, 227; Johnson, *St. Mark*, 127; see also Swete, *St Mark*, 139.

Especially difficult to interpret is the clause, "He meant to pass by (*ēthelen parelthein*) them" (vs. 48). The central problem: why Jesus should intend to go *by* the boat. Various explanations for his motive have been advanced, but most are conjectural and less than satisfactory; they are summarized in Johnson, *St. Mark*, 127; Montefiore, *Mark*, 127; Taylor, *St. Mark*, 329. The wording is best understood as highlighting the character of the narrative as epiphany: Jesus wished to reveal his power and glory to the disciples. If that interpretation is correct, then the infinitive *parelthein* would be as well if not better translated "pass before." It has been suggested that there is an allusion here to the theophanies in the LXX, when Yahweh passed before Moses on Sinai (Ex 33:19,22) and Elias on Horeb (1 Kgs 19:11–12): so Ernst Lohmeyer, *Das Evangelium des Markus*, Kritisch-exegetischer Kommentar über das Neue Testament, begründet von Heinrich August Wilhelm Meyer (12th ed.; Göttingen: Vandenhoeck & Ruprecht, 1953) 133. The verb *pererchesthai* being a common one, however, this proposal can only be tentative.

29. Martin Dibelius, *From Tradition to Gospel* (tr. Bertram Lee Woolf from 2nd German ed.; New York: Scribner's, 1935 [1st German ed., 1919]) 277.

30. Rudolf Bultmann, *Synoptic Tradition*, 230.

31. Loisy, *Evangiles*, I, 941–42; and *Marc*, 201–202.

32. Lohmeyer, *Markus*, 135–36.

to be a ghost and in Jesus' words of reassurance (vs. 49–50), motifs which appear in the resurrection accounts (Mt 28:10; Lk 24:37–39; cf. Mk 16:5–8). The point of the story, Loisy says, is that it is patterned on the passion and resurrection narratives in recounting Jesus' departure, the disciples' distress, and Jesus' return in glory.

Loisy suggests, moreover, that the two narratives look forward to the final departure and return, the parousia. He thus sees homiletic overtones in the story; the Church, in the midst of trials, is exhorted to await in faith and hope the certain coming of the Lord. Other commentators[33] also, while not following Loisy in other respects, interpret the narrative along homiletic lines.

Such are various meanings which have been found in these stories. The task at hand is to draw from them a coherent and sound interpretation of the miracles. Quite possibly the key to an understanding lies in discerning the relation between the two. Perhaps they were handed down as a pair in the tradition, since they are juxtaposed also in the Gospel of John. But whether they were joined in Mark's source or by Mark himself, they are certainly meant to be taken together as they stand in the Gospel. If the disciples were terrified at the sight of Jesus walking on the sea (vss. 49–50), it was because of their inability to recognize him, which in turn was owing to their failure to have grasped the meaning of the feeding. That is explicitly stated in the editorial comment which brings the two stories to a close: "And they were utterly astounded [at Jesus' walking on the waves] for they did not understand about the loaves, but their hearts were hardened" (vss. 51b–52). The redaction-critical question therefore arises out of the Markan narrative: what in the first miracle would have yielded the clue to the second, or how are the two related? The question must be addressed at two levels, that of the disciples within the story, and that of the readers of Mark's Gospel.

One answer is that the connection lies in the common portrayal of Jesus as Lord of the natural elements: he who could feed a multitude from a few loaves and fishes could as well exercise mastery over wind and wave.[34] This interpretation, however, falls short of adequately explaining the important theme of the disciples' incomprehension. Another answer has to do with the identity of Jesus: the disciples ought to have grasped in the feeding miracle the secret of Jesus' person; they would not then have failed to believe in his divine power over the water.[35] This interpretation is more satisfactory, but it still leaves unanswered the crucial question as to what in the feeding miracle would reveal specifically Jesus' identity and mission.

The answer very likely is to be found in an important theme of biblical and

---

33. E.g., Cranfield, *Saint Mark*, 228-29; Nineham, *St Mark*, 181; Rawlinson, *St Mark*, 88; Taylor, *St. Mark*, 330.

34. Johnson, *St. Mark*, 126.

35. Cranfield, *Saint Mark*, 227; Lagrange, *Saint Marc*, 175.

related theology. This is the expectation that the eschatological event would be a repetition of the Exodus and wandering.[36] An OT example of such speculation appears in the prophecies of Second Isaiah (chs. 35, 40ff.) of a new and greater Exodus to come.[37] There is also evidence that in Judaism in NT times Moses was regarded as a type of the Messiah, and the miracle of the manna was expected to occur again in the coming age (2 Apoc. Bar. 29:8; Sib. Or. frag. 3:46–49; Midrash Qoheleth Rabba on Eccl 1:9; Midrash Tanḥuma, Ḃšallaḥ 21; Mekilta on Ex 16:25; for the Exodus typology in the NT, see 1 Cor 10:1–5). The idea of the end-time as a new Exodus of salvation illuminates the Markan miracles of the loaves.

The disciples (and readers) ought to have perceived in the feeding the repetition of the miracle of the manna. The event affords, in sum, a glimpse into the mystery of the kingdom of God. It signifies that the new Exodus and redemptive event has begun. The Markan miracle intends to teach that a greater than Moses and the prophets is here, indeed, that Jesus is the fulfillment of the law and the prophets, the agent of God's final saving act in history.

On this interpretation, the second miracle comes as a fitting climax to the first. Both disclose who Jesus is: the first is a veiled revelation, given to the disciples and the crowd; the second an epiphany, given to the disciples alone. Had the disciples penetrated the mystery of the first, they would not have been utterly confounded at the demonstration of Jesus' power and glory in the second.

Mark's readers are intended to see, from their post-Easter perspective, yet further meaning.[38] For them the pair of miracles bears a twofold allusion, to the Exodus, and to the passion and resurrection of Jesus.[39] The miracles tie together the first and the final redemptive events; for Christians Jesus' death and resurrection is the moment in history which is the point of departure for the new Exodus. If the miracle of the loaves points to the Last Supper (6:41;

36. The importance of the Exodus for Jewish and Christian speculations of the first century concerning the end-time is stressed by Harald Sahlin, "The New Exodus of Salvation According to St Paul," in The Root of the Vine: Essays in Biblical Theology (ed. A. G. Hebert; New York: Philosophical Library, 1953) 81–95.

37. It is interesting to note in these chapters of Isaiah the motifs of wilderness (40:3; 43:19–20), divine power over the waters (43:2,16), the shepherd feeding his flock (40:11), deafness and blindness (42:16,18–20; 43:8), and the phrases "I am he" (41:4; 43:10,13,25) and "fear not" (35:4; 41:10).

38. The meaning of these miracles (and of other Markan passages) for the readers of the Gospel is thoroughly explored in Quentin Quesnell, The Mind of Mark: Interpretation and Method through the Exegesis of Mark 6,52, AnBib 38 (Rome: Pontifical Biblical Institute, 1969). Quesnell emphasizes especially the eucharistic allusion in the feeding miracles, and proposes an interpretation much like that of the present study in its main lines.

39. Possibly the notations of time in the two miracle stories, the meal in the evening and the appearance early in the morning (6:35 and 6:48), are meant to parallel those of the Last Supper and the discovery of the empty tomb (14:17 and 16:2; cf. Ex 16:6b-7a).

14:22), a Passover meal, it is not unreasonable to infer that it suggests also its context, the passion. Christians know that at both meals the bread which is broken and distributed that those who partake may have life is Jesus' body. That the sea miracle suggests the resurrection is clear enough from the biblical symbolism of water, the motifs which recur in the resurrection stories, and the glorious appearance of Jesus. The passion-resurrection foreshadowing provides the most satisfactory explanation available for the joining of these two miracles in Mark. What the readers are urged to understand is the relation between the two miracles: the breaking of the bread, symbol of Jesus' death, precedes the victory over waters, symbol of his resurrection. Then, the section 6:30–8:26 teaches in an obscure manner what is said plainly in 8:27–10:45:[40] it is through death that the Messiah gives the gift of new life. The readers are asked to acknowledge Jesus' messiahship in the cross as in the empty tomb.

For Mark's audience the miracle of the loaves would as well be a foreshadowing of the eucharist. What was given to the crowd in the feeding—the new manna, with all that that implies—is made available to Christians in the Lord's Supper.[41] The Christian readers are here enjoined above all to recognize the presence of Jesus in their eucharistic meals.[42] The miraculous feeding and the eucharist together also anticipate the messianic banquet, these points being connected by the thread of the eschatological theme; at the celebration of the Lord's Supper of course Christians await Jesus' return—or, what is evidently the same in Mark, the appearance of the Risen One—with heightened expectation. On this reading, the allusion in the sea miracle to the parousia and its homiletic lesson for Mark's community, which is experiencing adversity, is quite evident.

Mk 8:1–21

The second miracle of the loaves and fish, the feeding of the four thousand (8:1–10), has much the same meaning as the first; a detailed exegesis is therefore not required. As the first feeding was followed by a dispute with the Pharisees and scribes concerning ritual vs. ethical purity (7:1–23), so this one is followed immediately by an argument with the Pharisees concerning a sign (8:11–13).

40. So Johnson, St. Mark, 126; Lohmeyer, Markus, 136.

41. Quesnell, Mind of Mark, 232, 257, outlines those things which could be summed up as "eucharistic" for Mark's readers: the breaking of bread at the community meals, Jesus' passion and death, the expectation of his second coming, the union of Jew and Gentile in one way of salvation, and the experience of the Lord's presence in the community.

42. Quesnell, Mind of Mark, 264, connects Mk 6:52 with Lk 24:31,35, where Jesus is made known to the disciples at Emmaus "in the breaking of the bread." He suggests that the idea of recognizing Jesus in the breaking of the bread was a universal tradition in the early Church.

The Pharisees demand a "sign" from Jesus (vs. 11), by which they mean no doubt some astounding display from heaven which will authenticate his works (cf. 13:4,22). The scribes had earlier accused Jesus of performing exorcisms by Beelzebul (3:22); the Pharisees now pose essentially the same question as the leaders in Jerusalem will later ask: "By what authority are you doing these things, or who gave you this authority to do them?" (11:28). What they seek is verification of the eschatological proclamation expressed in Jesus' ministry, or, in other words, ratification of the claim to authority implicit in all his words and deeds. They demand, in sum, unmistakable proof of Jesus' messiahship. They seek such a sign, Mark says, "to test" Jesus (vs. 11). As comparison with 10:2 and 12:15 shows, the verb is equivalent to "entrap": the Pharisees challenge Jesus on the supposition that he will either accede and fail to produce the sign, or refuse and lose his popularity with the people.[43]

Jesus rejects the demand outright. The ground for his refusal undoubtedly is that they have in fact been given signs, especially in the loaves, which their spiritual blindness has rendered them incapable of perceiving. Then, this narrative, like Mark 4, has to do with the central issue of faith. Were the Pharisees given signs of the kind they sought, faith would be precluded; if they possessed faith, they would understand that signs had been given them, not of their own design but of God's. Such exegetical discourse employs, of course, two uses of the term "sign": the Pharisaic and Markan use, meaning an obvious demonstration of the eschatological divine presence (as in 13:4,22); and the Johannine use, an act conveying a veiled revelation.[44]

The language of Mark suggests that the reader is to recall the hardness of heart of the Israelites during the wandering. "This generation" (vs. 12), by which is probably meant the Pharisees as typifying the Jewish people, is like the infamous "generation" of the Exodus led by Moses.[45] Then Yahweh had spoken of "the men who have seen my glory and my signs which I wrought in Egypt and the wilderness, and yet have put me to the proof these ten times and have not hearkened to my voice" (Num 14:22); and later through the psalmist Yahweh had recalled the time "when your fathers tested me, and put me to the proof, though they had seen my work" (Ps 95:9 [LXX 94:9]; cf. Ex 4:8–9; 17:2,7; Num 14:11; Dt 13:1; 29:2–4; Isa 7:10–14; 38:7).

The miracles, like the parables, are revelations given obliquely. Those who will not see and hear identify themselves by their very obstinacy as "those outside" to whom "the secret of the kingdom," or signs, will not be given. The pericope is thus parallel to 4:10–12, with its paradoxical theme of obduracy, both predetermined and willful; and the following pericope, in

---

43. So Taylor, *St. Mark*, 362.

44. Cf. "sign" at Mt 12:39; 16:4; Lk 11:16,29.

45. The term "generation," usually pejorative, occurs in Dt 1:35; 32:5; Ps 95:10 [LXX 94:10]; Mk 8:38; 9:19; 13:30; Mt 11:16; 12:39; 16:4; Lk 11:29; Acts 2:40; Phil 2:15.

which Jesus attempts to open the disciples' eyes to the meaning of the loaves, is parallel to 4:13-20, where the parable is explained to them.

The following passage (vss. 14-21), while important, is exceptionally cryptic. Jesus embarks with his disciples who, we are told, had forgotten to bring bread and "had only one loaf with them in the boat" (vs. 14). Since the latter statement seems gratuitous in the context of the narrative, it has been suggested that it bears an indirect meaning, namely a reference to Jesus, the one true bread, a metaphor which would have been grasped by Mark's readers.[46]

Jesus says to the disciples, "Take heed, beware of the leaven of the Pharisees and the leaven of Herod" (vs. 15). The crux of the saying, the word "leaven," has been variously interpreted. Some[47] understand it as the threat represented by these two parties to the safety of the disciples (cf. 3:6; 12:13); this interpretation, however, leaves vs. 15 unrelated to the rest of the passage, except on the superficial level of a catchword association. Others,[48] probably more accurately, take the word "leaven" to mean an evil, pervasive influence, as the word connotes. Possibly it represents a this-worldly, nationalist idea of the kingdom;[49] or perhaps the leaven of the Pharisees stands for their legalistic, cultic-ritual piety (as in 7:1-23), and the leaven of Herod for kingly and political concerns.[50] (Cf. Mt 16:12, where it is interpreted as the teaching of the Pharisees and Sadducees; and Lk 12:1, as the Pharisees' hypocrisy.) Whatever the specific sense of the metaphor, which is virtually impossible to determine, the saying calls to mind the Pharisees in the immediately preceding pericope (vss. 11-13), and suggests therefore the general attitude that issues in the unbelief demonstrated there. It has to do, in fine, with the resistance of "those outside" to acknowledging Jesus' eschatological status. Then, in vs. 15, Jesus warns his disciples, and especially Mark's readers, to put away the blindness that would hinder their recognition of him.

The use of the term "leaven" is deliberate here; it alludes to the leaven which was to be put away during Passover or the Feast of Unleavened Bread (Ex 12:14-20; cf. Ex 13:3-10; 23:18; Lev 2:11). Its effect therefore is to continue the themes of the feeding miracles: to a Christian reader, an allusion to Passover would suggest not only the Exodus but Jesus' death and

46. Quesnell, *Mind of Mark*, 242-43.

47. Hunter, *Saint Mark*, 86.

48. Cranfield, *Saint Mark*, 260; Gould, *St. Mark*, 146; Johnson, *St. Mark*, 143; Lagrange, *Saint Marc*, 208; Loisy, *Evangiles*, I, 1001; and *Marc*, 231; Nineham, *St Mark*, 215; Schmid, *Mark*, 150; Swete, *St Mark*, 169; Taylor, *St. Mark*, 365.

49. So Schmid, *Mark*, 150-51.

50. So Cranfield, *Saint Mark*, 261; Gould, *St. Mark*, 146; Johnson, *St. Mark*, 143-44; Lagrange, *Saint Marc*, 208; Loisy, *Evangiles*, I, 1001; and *Marc*, 231; C. F. D. Moule, *The Gospel According to Mark*, The Cambridge Bible Commentary: New English Bible (Cambridge: Cambridge University Press, 1965) 62; Swete, *St Mark*, 169-70.

resurrection as well. The association of a warning against leaven and the idea of Christ as paschal lamb is explicit in 1 Cor 5:6–8 (cf. Mk 14:12).

In vs. 16, the disciples do display a degree of obtuseness; they respond to Jesus' saying about leaven by discussing the trivial fact that they "have no bread." A word which Jesus had intended metaphorically is interpreted by them in a simple, literal sense, and again we have the inability or unwillingness of the hearers to apprehend tropical meaning. Mark is of course employing a device fully developed in the Gospel of John, in which the hearers' merely literal understanding of a symbolic word gives occasion for deeper explanation by Jesus.

As we learn from vss. 17–21, however, the disciples' incomprehension has to do only incidentally with the saying about leaven; what the disciples do not grasp, much more importantly, is the meaning of the loaves. That the verses on this subject comprise one of the longest utterances of Jesus in Mark's Gospel is an indication of their importance. The disciples are so sharply rebuked for not understanding that the prophet's words applied earlier to the outsiders (4:12) are here addressed, as a rhetorical question, to them: "Having eyes do you not see, and having ears do you not hear?" (vs. 18; cf. Isa 6:9–10; Jer 5:21; Ezek 12:2). Jesus then reminds them in detail of the two feedings, concluding, "Do you not yet understand?" (vs. 21). The challenging questions, of course, are directed primarily to the Christian audience.

The meaning of the loaves was discussed above in the interpretation of the first feeding miracle; but the evangelist draws out further meaning here. In recalling the two feedings (vss. 19–21), Jesus emphasizes the numbers and uses the two words for "basket" appearing in the two stories, thus preserving the distinctive features of the narratives themselves; there must therefore be some significance attached to these. The suggestion is probably correct that the two miracles signify salvation to Jews and Gentiles respectively. If so, in the first story the number twelve represents the twelve apostles, and *kophinos* (6:43; 8:19) denotes a basket commonly used by Jews; in the second narrative the number seven represents the Hellenistic deacons (Acts 6:1–6) and *spuris* (8:8,20) denotes an ordinary basket.[51] Corroboration for such an exegesis is provided by the structure of this section of the Gospel (chs. 6–8), which carefully traces the movement of Jesus from the Jewish to the Gentile world, and which evidently situates the first feeding in Jewish, the second in Gentile, territory.[52] In this passage the readers and disciples are called upon to understand the universal destiny of the Gospel. Jesus' death is

---

51. So Bowman, *Mark*, 174–77; Cranfield, *Saint Mark*, 223 (tentatively); Loisy, *Evangiles*, I, 1005; and *Marc*, 225–28, 234–35; Montefiore, *Mark*, 177; Rawlinson, *St Mark*, 86; Taylor, *St. Mark*, 357.

52. The sequence of events is as follows: the feeding of the five thousand (6:30–52), Jesus works miracles (6:53–56), the debate with the Jews on cultic-ritual *vs.* ethical purity (7:1–23), Jesus' departure into the region of Tyre and Sidon (7:24), the Syrophoenician woman (7:25–30),

the sacrifice of the new covenant (14:24) by which a community is instituted composed of Jews and Gentiles whose fellowship is realized in their breaking bread together. As in the case of Jesus' abrogation of food laws (7:15,18–23), the motif of the disciples' incomprehension is made effective by the fact that the Gentile mission developed in the post-Easter history of the Church.

Again, the incident which immediately follows is closely tied to this episode. The miracle at Bethsaida in which a blind man is gradually healed (8:22–26) is a "sign" of coming to faith, and illustrates the great Markan theme of seeing, understanding, or believing. There follows the climactic event of Peter's confession at Caesarea Philippi (8:27–30) in which the eyes of the disciples are opened to the recognition of Jesus as Messiah. The first part of the Gospel, with its striking use of the device of veiled revelation, comes to a close, and the second part begins, with its explicit teaching on suffering, death, and resurrection.

Miracles and Parables

It is now well established that the Synoptic miracles, by and large, are to be understood eschatologically.[53] The exorcisms, healings, and other miracles themselves bring the blessings of the kingdom. The miracles are presented in the Synoptic Gospels at least partly as the fulfillment of OT prophecies and Jewish expectations regarding the new age. It is also generally agreed that the miracles sometimes function as "signs" even in the Synoptics, that is, that they point to realities beyond themselves.[54] That means, essentially, that what a miracle effects in the physical order has its analogy in the spiritual: the healing of the paralytic (Mk 2:1–12), for instance, signifies the forgiveness of sin; as noted, the miracle performed for the Syrophoenician woman (Mk 7:24–30) signifies salvation to the Gentiles; and the healing of the blind man (Mk 8:22–26), the spiritual seeing, or faith, enjoined throughout Mark's Gospel.

---

the healing of the deaf-mute in the region of the Decapolis (7:31–37), and the feeding of the four thousand (8:1–21).

53. The eschatological significance of the Synoptic miracles is emphasized by Robert M. Grant, *Miracle and Natural Law in Graeco-Roman and Early Christian Thought* (Amsterdam: North-Holland, 1952) esp. 165–72; and Edwyn Hoskyns and Noel Davey, *The Riddle of the New Testament* (London: Faber paperback ed., 1958) esp. 117–26.

54. The following works discuss the Synoptic miracles as "signs" in the Johannine sense: Raymond E. Brown, Ch. 10: "The Gospel Miracles," *New Testament Essays* (Milwaukee, Wis.: Bruce, 1965) 168–91 (a reprint of the essay in *The Bible in Current Catholic Thought* [ed. John L. McKenzie; New York: Herder, 1963] 184–201); John M. Court, "The Philosophy of the Synoptic Miracles," *JTS* 23 (1972) 1–15; Reginald H. Fuller, *Interpreting the Miracles* (London: SCM Press, 1963); Alan Richardson, *The Miracle-Stories of the Gospels* (London: SCM Press, 1941). See also Mark Erroll Glasswell, "The Use of Miracles in the Markan Gospel," in *Miracles: Cambridge Studies in Their Philosophy and History* (ed. C. F. D. Moule; London: Mowbray, 1965) 149–62.

The implication of these insights for the relation of miracle to parable, however, has not been clearly spelled out in the literature on miracles. The conclusion to which this proper view of the miracles leads is that they are like the parables in an important way, that of the double-meaning effect. In the miracles of the loaves, we have on one level simply the miraculous feeding of a crowd of people, and on another the suggestion that what is taking place here is the momentous event of the new Exodus and manna expected with the dawning of the kingdom. Thus the problem of the disciples' incomprehension can, as in the case of the parables, arise: what occurs is their failure to grasp the indirect but real meaning of the miracles, their eschatological significance. It is not necessary to strain this observation to the point of calling the miracles acted parables. A parable is always a literary composition, a verbal artifact; a miracle is an action or event. Parables and miracles are quite different phenomena and nothing is gained by confounding them. It is important, however, to know that the miracles, as they are treated in Mark, are similar to the parables in having more than one level of meaning and are thus subject to the same misunderstanding as the parables. It is this aspect of the miracles which Mark underscores for the reader in 6:52 and 8:17–21.

C. CONCLUSIONS: THE MYSTERY OF THE KINGDOM

These concluding remarks address three questions which arise out of the preceding discussion: (1) What light can the parables shed on the secret of the kingdom of God? (2) In what sense, precisely, are the parables mysterious in Mark's Gospel? and (3) How was it possible for Mark to treat in a similar manner such diverse things as parable, wisdom saying, and miracle? The summary and conclusions tendered here will show, perhaps, that a correct understanding of the parable is an important, if not the most important, way into the understanding of Mark's redaction.

The Secret of the Kingdom of God

A thorough and systematic treatment of the problem of the messianic secret lies outside the scope of the present study; nevertheless a few observations on the mystery motif as it is related to the parables may be in order.[55] In recent decades it has often been noted that, Wrede notwithstanding, the theme of mystery in Mark is broader than the "messianic secret," or the secret of Jesus' identity. To speak as though all the secrecy passages are messianic or Christological is to distort the problem; it is more accurate to speak generally of mystery, and to see Jesus' messianic role as one of its

---

55. I am indebted to William R. Schoedel for a number of these observations on the Markan mystery motif.

elements. The mystery to which Jesus refers at Mk 4:11 is not strictly Christological: it is "the secret of the kingdom of God."[56] Jesus says that this secret is given to those outside in parables (4:11). A reasonable procedure, then, in the quest for the secret, is to examine the parables themselves and the wisdom saying and miracle stories that function as they do. Perhaps the most important conclusion to emerge from such an examination is that, despite the diversity of subjects, all of these pericopes touch in one way or another on the theme of humility and suffering.

The hidden meaning of the sower (4:1-9) has to do with the cost of hearing and keeping the word: the private interpretation (4:13-20) shows that "tribulation" and "persecution" and "the cares of the world" must be overcome. The programmatic first parable, then, expresses one element of the mystery, the requirement for the disciple to "deny himself and take up his cross" (8:34). The similitudes of the growing seed and the mustard seed (4:26-32) are about unpropitious beginnings in the work of Jesus: they teach that precisely through what is insignificant the kingdom comes. Another programmatic parable, the wicked tenants (12:1-12, not treated in the exegetical parts of this study), has an unmistakable reference to Jesus' passion (vss. 7-8).

The hidden meaning of the wisdom saying on what defiles (7:15-23) is the insight that Jewish food laws are irrelevant. Mark represents Jesus as rejecting not Judaism entirely but its obduracy, especially that of the scribes and Pharisees. Theirs is a system that cannot break out of a repressive ritual to serve the sick (2:1-12; 3:1-6), the sinners (2:15-17), the hungry (2:23-28). The Jewish leaders reject the Son of God (12:1-12). Their piety does not recognize the role of humility (12:38-44). In sum, official Judaism cannot accept the way of service and suffering which is the mystery of the kingdom.

The miracles of the loaves also have a hidden meaning (6:30-44,52; 8:1-10,14-21): they refer to a view of the messiahship which involves suffering. This is shown by the connection between the miracles and the Last Supper (6:41; 8:6; 14:22-25). The historical point of departure of the new Passover is Jesus' death. Jesus is the one bread which is broken and given to both Jews and Gentiles (8:14-21), and the universalism hinted at in the wisdom saying at 7:15 is further developed (cf. 13:10). The Pharisees' idea of the messiahship which refuses to accept suffering results in the rejection of Judaism (8:11-13,15; cf. 11:27-33). It is the story of the Syrophoenician woman (7:25-30) that ties together the themes of food, the repudiation of Israel, and the Gentile mission which run through chs. 6-8.

The "secret of the kingdom of God," then, has to do with the necessity of suffering. This mystery is elucidated in the second half of the Gospel. The remark that Jesus "said this plainly" (8:32) at the outset of the second part,

---

56. The distinction between the messianic secret and the mystery of the kingdom is discussed by Schuyler Brown, "'The Secret of the Kingdom of God' (Mark 4:11)," *JBL* 92 (1973) 60-74.

where he begins to speak of suffering, shows that this is the same as the teaching conveyed "in parables" (4:11) in the first half. The dividing point in the Gospel is the confession of Peter that Jesus is "the Christ" (8:29)—a pericope bracketed by two revelatory events, the healing of the blind man (8:22–26) and the transfiguration of Jesus on the mountain (9:2–8). Just at this moment of the clearest revelation the mystery is disclosed: the coming of the kingdom with power (9:1) presupposes the suffering of the Son of man (8:31–33; cf. 9:12,30–32; 10:32–34; 14:25). The basic paradox is that he who teaches and works miracles with "authority" (1:22,27; 2:10; 6:7; 11:28ff.) is the one who must suffer and die. This gives meaning to the present suffering of Christians: the path to victory is through renunciation and trial (8:34–38; 10:35–45; cf. 9:33–37). Only in this way does the kingdom of God come. The stress here is on the understanding of the role that suffering may play in the lives of the Christians.[57]

The mystery in Mark's Gospel has a dual purpose;[58] it functions in one way for "those outside" and in another for the disciples. The first purpose is the easier to describe, since it is spelled out in Mk 4:11–12, the only passage in the Gospel which explains the secrecy. The mystery of the kingdom is not given to the outsiders, who represent Judaism, because such is not God's plan. Mark therefore puts the mystery theme at the service of a theological explanation for Israel's rejection of the Messiah and God's rejection of Israel, and deals with the same problem as Paul in Romans 9–11 (see esp. Rom 11:8,25).

The second purpose is somewhat more complex. The disciples represent the Church, or Mark's readers. Those outside comprehend nothing about the mystery of the kingdom, for which they are excluded from repentance (4:11–12; 8:11–13). The disciples, in the person of Peter, come to perceive the *fact* of Jesus' messiahship (8:29, he is the "Christ," as the Church confesses), but they do not understand its *mode* or its meaning for them, even after Jesus' open declaration that "the Son of man must suffer . . . and be killed" (8:31).[59] The two levels of the mystery are revealed in the account of Peter's confession (8:27–30,31–33); for their failure to grasp the deeper level, the disciples are castigated (8:33; cf. 4:13; 6:52; 7:18; 8:17–21). In part the disciples' incomprehension points up the fact that this mystery could not be fully apprehended before the resurrection—though again, despite their

---

57. Similar conclusions regarding the secret of the kingdom are reached by G. Minette de Tillesse, *Le secret messianique dans l'Evangile de Marc, LD* 47 (Paris: Editions du Cerf, 1968).

58. These observations on the purpose of the Markan theme of mystery follow the thesis of David J. Hawkin, "The Incomprehension of the Disciples in the Marcan Redaction," *JBL* 91 (1972) 491–500.

59. The fact and the mode of Jesus' messiahship are distinguished in T. A. Burkill, Ch. 1: "The Hidden Son of Man in St. Mark's Gospel," *New Light on the Earliest Gospel: Seven Markan Studies* (Ithaca, N.Y.: Cornell University Press 1972) 1–38; and in Hawkin, "Incomprehension."

limited vision, the disciples act as the bearers of authentic tradition about Jesus' ministry. Its main purpose, however, is to bring into relief what the Christian readers are urged to understand: the mystery of suffering. We have here, as Hawkin [60] has pointed out, a typology *per contrarium*: what the disciples do not comprehend is precisely what the Church is called upon to accept.

The parables, wisdom saying, and miracle stories likewise operate in a dual way. On the one hand, being difficult to comprehend, they help to show why those outside failed to recognize the messiahship of Jesus. On the other, being extraordinary speech, they are a striking and memorable way of expressing the teaching of Jesus to the disciples and readers. Moreover, since these narratives convey indirect meaning which eludes even the disciples, their questions provide the occasion for Jesus to explain his teaching and so further to impress the hearers. Tropical meaning is thus a rhetorical device which Mark uses with great subtlety and effectiveness.

The Mysterious Parable

In an earlier chapter, the parable was defined as a tropical narrative, and it was pointed out that the double meaning of a parable is what makes possible its functioning as mysterious speech. This occurs when the hearer, for whatever reason, does not apprehend its indirect but more important level of meaning. Mark, like others before him in the Semitic tradition, has put the parable to this use. One result of the present study is *to minimize the distance between the parable as a literary construct and Mark's use of the parable*. The charge made in much of the scholarly literature since the nineteenth century that Mark has distorted the parable as a verbal construct is simply unfounded. Mark has not taken clear, straightforward speech, the parable, and transformed it into obscure, esoteric speech, the allegory. He has rather taken what is essential to the parable, the double-meaning effect, and made it the starting point of a theological theme concerning the audience's resistance to hearing the word.

The theological, as distinct from the literary, aspect of the Markan mystery remains to be described more precisely. Even a brief survey such as that in the preceding section reveals that the tropical meaning of the Markan parables cannot be called a mystery of doctrine; the parables are not esoteric sayings in the usual sense of that term. What the parables (and wisdom saying and miracles) teach are the implications of the coming of the kingdom for the situation of the audience. They convey not secret information, but the requirements made of the hearer. The mystery has to do entirely with one's willingness to receive the eschatological and ethical teaching of Jesus. The word "willingness" is deliberately used here: Mark's theory is that the meaning of a parable is perceived only by those disposed to appropriate its

60. Hawkin, "Incomprehension," 500.

teaching; those who do not understand are those who will not allow its lesson to impinge on their own existence.

The mystery in Mark's Gospel is not a mystery of dogma, but a mystery of application—or, to use the words of Robinson,[61] not an intellectual, but an existential mystery. In the Gospel of Mark understanding is not so much knowledge as faith and obedience; and incomprehension is a matter not of intellectual obtuseness but of hardness of heart. The biblical concept "hardness of heart"—used twice in Mark in connection with the failure to understand (6:52; 8:17)—belongs to moral rather than dogmatic theology.

To say this, however, is not to drive a wedge between the meaning and the application of a parable, as though these were two different things. T. W. Manson has said that a hearer may grasp the former and miss the latter;[62] that, however, is not precisely what happens in the parabolic speech acts in the Bible. Rather, the meaning and the application of a parable are one and the same; either both are accepted or both are repudiated. In Mark's Gospel, the hearers who fail to perceive a parable's meaning do so because they resist its application to their own situation. The term "mystery of application" is employed in the present study for the purpose of distinguishing the Markan mystery of the parables, which has to do with hardness of heart, from a mystery which has to do with secret knowledge.

The concept "hardness of heart," however, is not altogether simple. There is in this idea, as observed earlier, an interplay of the divine and human wills, a tension between determinism and freedom. Who ultimately causes the hardening of heart is not clear. It would be best, perhaps, to say that the parables are the means both by which God judges the hearers, and by which the hearers bring judgment upon themselves. That such speculation is not worked out in accordance with logic should not prevent the exegete from seeing that the notions of the divine plan and human responsibility are in fact brought together in Mark. Any interpretation of Mark 4 which observes either predestination or free will exclusively is not describing everything that is there.

61. James M. Robinson, *The Problem of History in Mark*, *SBT* 21 (London: SCM Press, 1957) 76.

62. T. W. Manson, *Teaching*, 64–66, cites as an example of the dichotomy between meaning and application Nathan's parable of the ewe lamb (2 Sam 12:1–7). On close examination, however, it can be seen that David fails to grasp not just the application but the meaning of the parable. He fails precisely to understand that it *is* a parable, having a tropical meaning referring to him; he takes it rather as a true story having only a literal meaning.

Robinson, *Problem of History*, 76, seems to follow Manson on this point. He cites two Markan parables (3:23; 12:1–12) which he says are "understood intellectually" but "repudiated existentially." Mark does not say of either of these parables, however, that they were not understood. On the contrary, following the wicked tenants (12:1–12) it is said that the Jewish leaders "perceived that he had told the parable against them" (vs. 12). What this means is simply that Mark does not employ this parable in the way he does others; he does not put it in the service of the mystery theme as he does those in ch. 4.

Parable, Wisdom Saying, and Miracle

Parable, wisdom saying, and miracle are, to be sure, very distinct things. A parable is a verbal construct, specifically a tropical narrative. A wisdom saying is also a verbal construct, but one quite different from the parable: it is a brief expository saying usually in parallel lines. A miracle is an event or a deed. Nevertheless these three, as they appear in the Gospel of Mark, all contribute to the theme of incomprehension. How they could be made to function in the same way was discussed in the preceding sections; the conclusions are here summarized.

It is essential to every parable, as has been emphasized in earlier chapters, that it have the double-meaning effect; a narrative cannot be a parable without a tropical as well as a literal sense. On the other hand, the double-meaning effect is not at all essential to the wisdom saying or miracle story; it *may*, however, occur in them.

The wisdom saying at Mk 7:15 can be presented by Mark as difficult to comprehend in part because it is based on circumlocution, which is less than direct and straightforward speech, and in part because it happens to employ an implicit trope. Mk 7:15 shares the devices of circumlocution and trope with many, though hardly all, biblical wisdom sayings. By exploiting these devices, Mark makes it possible for this wisdom saying to function as mysterious speech, and he thus brings it into line with the parables. Perhaps what led Mark to treat the wisdom saying as he did was the fact that in antiquity it too could be called *parabolē*, and it was occasionally regarded by the wisdom tradition as obscure (e.g., at Prov 1:5–6; Sir 39:2–3).

The double meaning is present in some, though not all, miracle stories; it occurs only in those which refer to a parallel spiritual reality. Some of the Markan miracles, as is generally recognized, are "signs" pointing to something outside themselves—and it is this indirect or second level of meaning which is of import. It is, again, by utilizing this double-meaning effect that Mark can present the miracles as analogous to the parables, and enable them to operate as mysterious phenomena. There is no tradition in the Semitic literature (as there is in the case of parables and wisdom sayings) of regarding miracles as mysterious; here Mark, or a predecessor, may be quite original. One feature in the OT, however, very likely contributed to the way in which miracles are treated in Mark's Gospel: that is the OT view of miracles wrought by God as "signs" (*ôth*; e.g., at Ex 4:8–9; 7:3; Num 14:11,22; Isa 7:10–14; 38:7). Especially illuminating are the words of Moses to Israel: "You have seen all that the Lord did before your eyes in the land of Egypt," he says, "the signs and those great wonders; but to this day the Lord has not given you a mind to understand, or eyes to see, or ears to hear" (Dt 29:2b,3b–4).

By thus fashioning the wisdom saying and miracle stories on the pattern of the parable, Mark gives to them the structure of indirect meaning—hence their mysteriousness.

APPENDIX

THE TERMS: CLASSICAL AND SEMITIC

This concise survey of relevant terms in the classical and Semitic literatures is included here for handy reference. More detailed treatments are available elsewhere.[1]

It should be noted here that the terms are not, and need not be, used in the same way in modern scholarly writing as in the ancient sources. On this point, see Chapter 2, Section A of this study.

A. CLASSICAL LITERATURE

Socrates

According to Aristotle (*Rhetoric* II.20.4) Socrates sometimes taught by means of the *parabolē*. One example of the Socratic *parabolē*, which occurs in the dialogue with Phaedrus, is interesting because of its resemblance to the parable of the sower. The subject of the entire dialogue is rhetoric; in this passage Socrates maintains the superiority of the spoken over the written word (*logos*). A husbandman, he says, would not when in earnest plant seeds in the summer heat in a garden of Adonis for quick but ephemeral growth, but carefully and in suitable ground for slow but lasting growth; just so the teacher will not when in earnest sow his words in ink, but orally so that they can be defended by argument and teach effectively (*Phaedrus* 61).

---

1. For the classical literature see the following: Lagrange, "La parabole," 198–212; Hermaniuk, *La parabole*, 35–61; and Hauck, "*parabolē*." Translations of the passages quoted here are from the Loeb Classical Library editions of Aristotle *The "Art" of Rhetoric* (tr. John Henry Freese); and Quintilian *The Institutio Oratoria of Quintilian* (tr. H. E. Butler).

For the Semitic literature see: Wilhelm Bacher, "*māšāl*," *Die exegetische Terminologie der jüdischen Traditionsliteratur* (Leipzig: Heinrichs'sche, 1899, 1905) Part I, pp. 121–22; Part II, p. 121; Marcus Jastrow, "*māšāl*," *A Dictionary of the Targumim, the Talmud Babli and Jerushalmi, and the Midrashic Literature*, I (New York: Putnam, 1903); Jacob Z. Lauterbach, "Parable," *The Jewish Encyclopedia*, IX (ed. Isidore Singer; New York: Funk & Wagnalls, 1905); Lagrange, "La parabole"; Allen Howard Godbey. "The Hebrew *Mašal*," *AJSL* 39 (1922–23) 89–108; Hermaniuk, *La parabole*, 62–189; Jean Pirot, "Le 'māšāl' dans l'Ancien Testament," *RSR* 37 (1950) 565–80; A. S. Herbert, "The 'Parable' (*Māšāl*) in the Old Testament," *SJT* 7 (1954) 180–96; A. R. Johnson, "*māšāl*," in *Wisdom in Israel and in the Ancient Near East*, VTSup 3 (Leiden: Brill, 1955) 162–69; C.-M. Edsman, G. Fohrer, E. L. Dietrich, N. A. Dahl, and K. Frör, "Gleichnis und Parabel," *RGG* II (3rd ed.); Augustin George, "Parabole," *DBSup* 6; L. Mowry, "Parable," *IDB* III; and Hauck, "*parabolē*."

Aristotle

Aristotle, in *The "Art" of Rhetoric*, discusses the various types of proofs available to the rhetorician. One of these is the example (*paradeigma*), which is divided into two kinds: the example taken from history and the example invented by the author. The invented example is in turn divided into two kinds: the *parabolē* (e.g., those of Socrates) and the *logos* (fable, e.g., those of Aesop). Aristotle does not define these terms; but he says it would be an example of the *parabolē*

> if one were to say that magistrates should not be chosen by lot, for this would be the same as choosing as representative athletes not those competent to contend, but those on whom the lot falls; or as choosing any of the sailors as the man who should take the helm, as if it were right that the choice should be decided by lot, not by a man's knowledge.

He gives as examples of the *logos* the fables of the horse, the stag and the man; and the fox, the fleas and the hedgehog (*Rhetoric* II.20).

Quintilian

Quintilian, in his work on rhetoric, the *Institutio Oratoria*, discusses the same two literary classes under their Latin names. The Latin word *similitudo*, he says, is equivalent to the Greek word *parabolē*. One example he gives is this *similitudo* of agricultural growth which also resembles some Synoptic parables: "if you wish to argue that the mind requires cultivation, you would use a comparison drawn from the soil, which if neglected produces thorns and thickets, but if cultivated will bear fruit." The Latin word *fabella* or *fabula*, he says, is equivalent to the Greek word *logos*; as an example he cites the fable of the limbs' quarrel with the belly, a fable based on the comparison of society to a body which is familiar to us from the writings of the Stoics and Paul (*Institutio* V.xi).

B. SEMITIC LITERATURE

Old Testament

The Hebrew word *māšāl* is usually translated in the LXX by the word *parabolē* (and occasionally by the word *paroimia*). The term *māšāl/parabolē* refers to a wide variety of literary classes. It sometimes designates a proverb (1 Sam 10:12; 24:13 [LXX 24:14]; Ezek 12:22-23; 16:44; 18:2-3). Elsewhere it appears to mean byword, a proverb in which a person or nation is held in derision (Dt 28:37; 1 Kgs 9:7; 2 Chr 7:20; Jer 24:9; Ezek 14:8; Tob 3:4; Wis 5:4). In two instances *māšāl/parabolē* denotes a taunt-song (Mic 2:4; Hab 2:6). In the Balaam stories it refers to blessings and curses (Num 23:7,18; 24:3,15,20,21,23). In Ezekiel the term refers three times to an extended comparison which functions as a prophetic oracle. The passages are those of the two eagles, the cedar and the vine (17:1-10, with explanation attached in vss. 11–21), followed by what is probably another comparison of the sprig that will become a noble cedar (vss. 22–24); the forest fire in the south (20:45–49 [LXX 21:2–5]); and the rusted cauldron (24:3–14, with explanation included).

The Book of Proverbs contains the word *māšāl* six times, three of which are in titles (1:1,6; 10:1; 25:1; 26:7,9). Here the term refers to the type of saying contained in the collection itself, the wisdom saying, usually composed of two or more parallel members of two stichs each. The Book of Sirach contains the same terms and the same type of saying (*parabolē* in 1:25; 3:29 [Hebr 3:27, *māšāl*]; 13:26; 20:20; 38:33; 39:2–3; 47:15 [*šîrâ*]; 47:17 [*ḥîdâ*]; and *paroimia* in 6:35 [*māšāl*]; 8:8; 18:29; 39:3; 47:17 [*mā[ša]l*]). Ecclesiastes contains two instances of the term *parabolē* (1:17 [no corresponding Hebr phrase]; 12:9 [*māšāl*]).

It may be that *māšāl/parabolē* denotes, in addition to wisdom sayings, the long poems that are found in Proverbs (e.g., in chs. 1-9) and Sirach (e.g., in ch. 24). Such a use of the term may occur also in the Psalms (49:4 [LXX 48:5]; 78:2 [LXX 77:2]) and in Job (27:1; 29:1). It is not possible to be more precise about the meaning of the word in these three instances.

There are nine OT passages which are usually included in discussions of the parable, although they are not called *mešālîm*. It is a matter of dispute whether the absence of the term in these cases is accidental or not. Three of these closely resemble the Synoptic parables: Nathan's ewe lamb (2 Sam 12:1–7); the wise woman of Tekoa's two brothers and the avengers (2 Sam 14:5–13); and the anonymous prophet's escaped prisoner (1 Kgs 20:39–42). Four are prophetic oracles: Isaiah's song of the vineyard (5:1–7); Isaiah's comparison of the farmer (28:23–29); and Ezekiel's lamentations of the lioness (19:1–9) and the vine (19:10–14). Two may be called fables: the trees choosing a king (Jgs 9:7–20); and the thistle and the cedar (2 Kgs 14:9–10). In most of these, the interpretation is either included or attached.

Finally, the term *māšāl/parabolē* may also have designated symbolic actions of the sort performed by the prophets. This meaning is nowhere unequivocally attested, but it need not for that reason be altogether discounted. Ezekiel's *māšāl* of the rusted cauldron (24:3–14), for example, may have been accompanied by such an act.

Apocalyptic Literature

In *1 Enoch* the Ethiopic term equivalent to the Hebrew *māšāl* denotes visions, or the descriptions of the visions, of heavenly realities and the end of days (e.g., 37:1; 38:1; 45:1; 58:1). It is not possible to determine whether the "parables" are the visions themselves, or the verbal accounts of them.

In *2 Esdras* the term *similitudo* in the Latin version once refers to an angel's proposition to Ezra which is impossible to carry out (e.g., to weigh fire). This is, the angel explains, a comparison: if Ezra cannot perform these earthly things, how then can he understand the ways of the Most High?

(4:3–11). Elsewhere in *2 Esdras* the term *similitudo* refers to a comparison in the form of a vision (4:44–50). There is one clear use of the term to denote a comparison in the form of a speech (8:1–3).

In the apocalyptic literature, the "parables" are difficult to comprehend and require interpretation by the angelic figure (e.g., *1 Enoch* 43:3–4; 46:2; *2 Esdras* 4:44–50).

Rabbinic Literature

The rabbinic writings exhibit the same variety of literary types under the term *māšāl* as do the OT and Intertestamental books. In the first century A.D. and later, then, the term continued to have a broad scope in meaning.

The rabbinic term *māšāl* sometimes refers to a proverb (e.g., *Midrash Tanḥuma, Maṭot* 5; *Midrash Eka Rabba*, proem 24). It frequently designates those extended comparisons which, as is well known, are quite like the Synoptic parables (e.g., *b. Pes* 49a; *Mekilta* on Ex 14:5; 15:1; *Pirqe Aboth* 3:20). Sometimes it denotes a fable (e.g., *b. Ber* 61b; *b. Suk* 28a; *b. Sanh* 38b). The rabbinic *māšāl* can also mean the allegorical interpretation of scripture; it is the twenty-sixth of the thirty-two modes of interpretation developed by R. Eliezer (*ca.* 200 A.D.). Finally, the term is sometimes used to point out that a person or story is fictitious; this is said, for example, of Job and of Ezekiel's story of the dry bones (*b. B B* 15a; *b. Erub* 63a; *b. Sanh* 92b).

BIBLIOGRAPHY

A. Books

Black, Matthew. *An Aramaic Approach to the Gospels and Acts.* 3rd ed. Oxford: Clarendon Press, 1967.

Brown, Raymond E. *The Semitic Background of the Term "Mystery" in the New Testament.* Philadelphia: Fortress Press, 1968.

Buber, Solomon, ed. *Midrasch Echa Rabbati.* Wilna: Wittwe & Gebrüder Romm, 1899.

_____. *Midrash Tanḥuma.* Wilna: Wittwe & Gebrüder Romm, 1885.

Bultmann, Rudolf. *The History of the Synoptic Tradition.* Tr. John Marsh. New York: Harper & Row, 1963.

Burkill, T. A. *Mysterious Revelation: An Examination of the Philosophy of St. Mark's Gospel.* Ithaca, N. Y.: Cornell University Press, 1963.

_____. *New Light on the Earliest Gospel: Seven Markan Studies.* Ithaca, N. Y.: Cornell University Press, 1972.

Burney, C. F. *The Poetry of Our Lord: An Examination of the Formal Elements of Hebrew Poetry in the Discourses of Jesus Christ.* Oxford: Clarendon Press, 1925.

Cadoux, A. T. *The Parables of Jesus: Their Art and Use.* London: Clarke, 1930.

Dibelius, Martin. *From Tradition to Gospel.* Tr. Bertram Lee Woolf. New York: Scribner's, 1935.

Dodd, C. H. *The Parables of the Kingdom.* rev. ed. New York: Scribner's, 1961.

Epstein, Isadore, ed. *The Babylonian Talmud.* 34 vols. London: Soncino Press, 1935–48.

Fiebig, Paul. *Altjüdische Gleichnisse und die Gleichnisse Jesu.* Tübingen: Mohr, 1904.

_____. *Die Gleichnisreden Jesu im Lichte der rabbinischen Gleichnisse des neutestamentlichen Zeitalters.* Tübingen: Mohr, 1912.

Fuller, Reginald H. *Interpreting the Miracles.* London: SCM Press, 1963.

Goldin, Judah, ed. and tr. *The Living Talmud: The Wisdom of the Fathers.* New York: New American Library, 1957.

Grant, Frederick C. *The Earliest Gospel.* New York: Abingdon Press, 1943.

Grant, Robert McQueen. *Miracle and Natural Law in Graeco-Roman and Early Christian Thought.* Amsterdam: North-Holland, 1952.

Hermaniuk, Maxime. *La parabole évangélique.* Louvain: Bibliotheca Alfonsiana, 1947.

Honig, Edwin. *Dark Conceit: The Making of Allegory.* New York: Oxford University Press, 1959.

Hoskyns, Edwyn and Davey, Noel. *The Riddle of the New Testament.* London: Faber paperback ed., 1958.

Jeremias, Joachim. *The Parables of Jesus.* rev. ed. Tr. S. H. Hooke. New York: Scribner's, 1963.

Jones, Geraint V. *The Art and Truth of the Parables.* Naperville, Ill.: Alec Allenson, 1964.

Jülicher, Adolf. *Die Gleichnisreden Jesu.* Vol. I: *Die Gleichnisreden Jesu im Allgemeinen.* Vol. II: *Auslegung der Gleichnisreden der drei ersten Evangelien.* Tübingen: Mohr; Vol. I, 2nd ed., 1899; Vol. II, 2nd ed., 1910.

Kingsbury, Jack Dean. *The Parables of Jesus in Matthew 13: A Study in Redaction-Criticism.* Richmond, Va.: John Knox, 1969.

Lauterbach, Jacob Z. *The Pharisees and Their Teachings.* New York: Bloch, 1930.

Linnemann, Eta. *Jesus of the Parables.* Tr. John Sturdy. New York: Harper & Row, 1966.

Manson, T. W. *The Teaching of Jesus: Studies of Its Form and Content.* 1st paperback ed. Cambridge: Cambridge University Press, 1963.

Minette de Tillesse, G. *Le secret messianique dans l'Evangile de Marc. LD* 47. Paris: Editions du Cerf, 1968.

Quesnell, Quentin. *The Mind of Mark: Interpretation and Method through the Exegesis of Mark 6,52. AnBib* 38. Rome: Pontifical Biblical Institute, 1969.

Richardson, Alan. *The Miracle-Stories of the Gospels.* London: SCM Press, 1941.

Robinson, James M. *The Problem of History in Mark. SBT* 21. London: SCM Press, 1957.

Russell, David Syme. *The Method and Message of Jewish Apocalyptic, 200 BC-AD 100.* Philadelphia: Westminster, 1964.

Schmidt, Karl Ludwig. *The Church.* Bible Key Words. Tr. J. R. Coates from *TWNT* II. London: Black, 1950.

Schweitzer, Albert. *The Mystery of the Kingdom of God.* Tr. Walter Lowrie. New York: Schocken Books, 1964.

———. *The Quest of the Historical Jesus.* Tr. W. Montgomery. New York: Macmillan, 1961.

Smith, B. T. D. *The Parables of the Synoptic Gospels.* Cambridge: Cambridge University Press, 1937.

Smith, Morton. *Tannaitic Parallels to the Gospels.* JBL Monograph Series, VI. Philadelphia: Society of Biblical Literature, 1951 (corrected reprint, 1968).

Vermes, Geza. *The Dead Sea Scrolls in English.* Baltimore: Penguin Books, 1962.

Via, Dan Otto, Jr. *The Parables: Their Literary and Existential Dimension.* Philadelphia: Fortress Press, 1967.

Weeden, Theodore J. *Mark: Traditions in Conflict.* Philadelphia: Fortress Press, 1971.

Wrede, Wilhelm. *The Messianic Secret.* Tr. J. C. G. Greig. London: Clarke, 1971.

B. Articles and Essays

Achtemeier, Paul J. "The Origin and Function of the Pre-Marcan Miracle Catenae," *JBL* 91 (1972) 198–221.

_____. "Toward the Isolation of Pre-Marcan Miracle Catenae," *JBL* 89 (1970) 265–91.

Bacher, Wilhelm. "*Māšāl.*" *Die exegetische Terminologie der jüdischen Traditionsliteratur*. Erster Teil: Die bibelexegetische Terminologie der Tannaiten. Zweiter Teil: Die bibel- und traditionsexegetische Terminologie der Amoräer. Leipzig: Heinrichs'sche, 1899, 1905.

Baird, J. Arthur. "A Pragmatic Approach to Parable Exegesis: Some New Evidence on Mark 4.11,33–34," *JBL* 76 (1957) 201–207.

Baumgärtel, Friedrich, and Behm, Johannes. "*kardia, kardiognōstēs, sklērokardia,*" *TDNT* III.

Baumgartner, W. "Die literarischen Gattungen in der Weisheit des Jesus Sirach," *ZAW* 34 (1914) 161–98.

Black, Matthew. "The Parables as Allegory," *BJRL* 42 (1959–60) 273–87.

Boobyer, G. H. "The Secrecy Motif in St. Mark's Gospel," *NTS* 6 (1960) 225–35.

Bornkamm, Günther. "*mystērion, myeō,*" *TDNT* IV.

Brown, Raymond E. Ch. 10: "The Gospel Miracles." *New Testament Essays*. Milwaukee, Wis.: Bruce, 1965. (A reprint of the essay in *The Bible in Current Catholic Thought*; ed. John L. McKenzie; New York: Herder, 1963.)

_____. Ch. 13: "Parable and Allegory Reconsidered." *New Testament Essays*. Milwaukee, Wis.: Bruce, 1965. (A reprint of the article in *NovT* 5 [1962] 36–45.)

_____. Ch. 7: "The Qumran Scrolls and the Johannine Gospel and Epistles." *New Testament Essays*. Milwaukee, Wis.: Bruce, 1965. (A reprint of the article in *CBQ* 17 [1955] 403–419, 559–74; and in *The Scrolls and the New Testament*; ed. Krister Stendahl; New York: Harper, 1957.)

Brown, Schuyler. " 'The Secret of the Kingdom of God' (Mark 4:11)," *JBL* 92 (1973) 60–74.

Burkill, T. A. "The Cryptology of Parables in St. Mark's Gospel," *NovT* 1 (1956) 246–62.

_____. "St. Mark's Philosophy of History," *NTS* 3 (1956–57) 142–48.

Cadbury, Henry J. "Soluble Difficulties in the Parables." *New Testament Sidelights: Essays in Honor of Alexander Converse Purdy*. Ed. Harvey K. McArthur. Hartford, Conn.: The Hartford Seminary Foundation Press, 1960.

Carlston, Charles Edwin. "A *Positive* Criterion of Authenticity?" *BR* 7 (1962) 33–44.

Cave, C. H. "The Parables and the Scriptures," *NTS* 11 (1964–65) 374–87.

Cerfaux, Lucien. " 'L'aveuglement d'espirit' dans l'Evangile de Saint Marc," *Le Muséon* (Mélanges L. Th. Lefort) 59 (1946) 267–79.

_____. "La connaissance des secrets du royaume d'après Mt., XIII,11 et parallèles," *Recueil L. Cerfaux*, III (1962) 123–38.

Court, John M. "The Philosophy of the Synoptic Miracles," *JTS* 23 (1972) 1–15.

Cranfield, C. E. B. "St. Mark 4.1–34," Part I, *SJT* 4 (1951) 398–414.

Crossan, John Dominic. "Parable and Example in the Teaching of Jesus," *NTS* 18 (1971–72) 285–307. (Reprinted in *Semeia* 1 [1974] 63–104.)

Dahl, Nils A. "The Parables of Growth," *ST* 5 (1952) 132–66.

Daube, David. "Public Pronouncement and Private Explanation in the Gospels," *ExpT* 57 (1945–46) 175–77.

———. Ch. 6: "Public Retort and Private Explanation." *The New Testament and Rabbinic Judaism*. London: University of London, Athlone Press, 1956.

Davies. W. D. " 'Knowledge' in the Dead Sea Scrolls and Matthew 11:25-30," *HTR* 46 (1953) 113–39.

Eakin, Frank E., Jr. "Spiritual Obduracy and Parable Purpose." *The Use of the Old Testament in the New and Other Essays: Studies in Honor of William Franklin Stinespring*. Ed. James M. Efird. Durham, N.C.: Duke University Press, 1972.

Edsman, C.-M., Fohrer, G., Dietrich, E. L., Dahl, N. A., and Frör, K. "Gleichnis und Parabel," *RGG* II. 3rd ed.

George, Augustin. "Parabole," *DBSup* 6.

———. "Le sens de la parabole des semailles (Mc., IV,3–9 et parallèles)," *Sac Pag* 2 (1959) 163–69.

Gerhardsson, Birger. "The Parable of the Sower and Its Interpretation." Tr. John Toy. *NTS* 14 (1967–68) 165–93.

Glasswell, Mark Erroll. "The Use of Miracles in the Markan Gospel." *Miracles: Cambridge Studies in Their Philosophy and History*. Ed. C. F. D. Moule. London: Mowbray, 1965.

Godbey, Allen Howard. "The Hebrew *Mašal*," *AJSL* 39 (1922–23) 89–108.

Hauck, Friedrich. "*parabolē*," *TDNT* V.

Hawkin, David J. "The Incomprehension of the Disciples in the Marcan Redaction," *JBL* 91 (1972) 491–500.

Herbert, A. S. "The 'Parable' (*Mašal*) in the Old Testament," *SJT* 7 (1954) 180–96.

Jastrow, Marcus. "*mašal*." *A Dictionary of the Targumim, the Talmud Babli and Jerushalmi, and the Midrashic Literature*, I. New York: Putnam, 1903.

Johnson, A. R. "*mašal*." *Wisdom in Israel and in the Ancient Near East. VTSup* 3. Leiden: Brill, 1955.

Koester, Helmut H. "One Jesus and Four Primitive Gospels," *HTR* 61 (1968) 203–47.

Lagrange, M.-J. "Le but des paraboles d'après l'Evangile selon Saint Marc," *RB* 2/7 (1910) 5–35.

———. "La parabole en dehors de l'Evangile," *RB* 2/6 (1909) 198–212, 342–67.

Lauterbach, Jacob Z. "Parable." *The Jewish Encyclopedia*, IX. Ed. Isidore Singer. New York: Funk & Wagnalls, 1905.

Manson, W. "The Purpose of the Parables: A Re-Examination of St. Mark iv.10–12," *ExpT* 68 (1956–57) 132–35.

Marxsen, Willi, "Redaktionsgeschichtliche Erklärung der sogenannten Parabeltheorie des Markus," *ZTK* 52 (1955) 255–71.

Moule, C. F. D. "Mystery," *IDB* III.

Mowry, L. "Parable," *IDB* III.

Perrin, Norman. "Historical Criticism, Literary Criticism, and Hermeneutics: The Interpretation of the Parables of Jesus and the Gospel of Mark Today," *JR* 52 (1972) 361–75.

_____. "The Modern Interpretation of the Parables of Jesus and the Problem of Hermeneutics," *Int* 25 (1971) 131–48.

_____. "The Parables of Jesus as Parables, as Metaphors, and as Aesthetic Objects: A Review Article," *JR* 47 (1967) 340–46.

_____. "Wisdom and Apocalyptic in the Message of Jesus." *Society of Biblical Literature 1972 Proceedings*, Vol. II, 543–72.

Pirot, Jean. "Le 'mašāl' dans l'Ancien Testament," *RSR* 37 (1950) 565–80.

Robinson, J. Armitage. "On *pōrōsis* and *pērōsis*." *St Paul's Epistle to the Ephesians.* London: Macmillan, 1903.

_____. "On the Meaning of *mystērion* in the New Testament." *St Paul's Epistle to the Ephesians.* London: Macmillan, 1903.

Robinson, James M. "The Problem of History in Mark, Reconsidered," *USQR* 20 (1964–65) 131–47.

Sahlin, Harald. "The New Exodus of Salvation According to St Paul." *The Root of the Vine: Essays in Biblical Theology.* Ed. A. G. Hebert. New York: Philosophical Library, 1953.

Schmidt, Karl Ludwig and Schmidt, Martin Anton. "*pachynō, pōroō (pēroō), pōrōsis (pērōsis), sklēros, sklērotēs, sklērotrachēlos, sklērynō,*" TDNT V.

Siegman, Edward F. "Teaching in Parables (Mk 4,10–12; Lk 8,9–10; Mt 13,10–15)," *CBQ* 23 (1961) 161–81.

Smith, Morton. "Comments on Taylor's Commentary on Mark," *HTR* 48 (1955) 21–64.

Stendahl, Krister. "The Called and the Chosen. An Essay on Election." *The Root of the Vine: Essays in Biblical Theology.* Ed. A. G. Hebert. New York: Philosophical Library, 1953.

Vogt, E. " 'Mysteria' in textibus Qumran," *Bib* 37 (1956) 247–57.

Weeden, Theodore J. "The Heresy That Necessitated Mark's Gospel," *ZNW* 59 (1968) 145–58.

C. Commentaries on the Gospel of Mark

Bowman, John. *The Gospel of Mark: The New Christian Jewish Passover Haggadah.* SPB 8. Leiden: Brill, 1965.

Branscomb, B. Harvie. *The Gospel of Mark.* The Moffatt New Testament Commentary. New York: Harper, 1937.

Cranfield, C. E. B. *The Gospel According to Saint Mark.* Cambridge Greek Testament Commentary. Cambridge: Cambridge University Press, 1959 (reprinted, with supplementary notes, 1963).

Gould, Ezra Palmer. *A Critical and Exegetical Commentary on the Gospel According to St. Mark.* International Critical Commentary. New York: Scribner's, 1896.

Grant, Frederick C. "The Gospel According to St. Mark." *The Interpreter's Bible*, VII. New York: Abingdon Press, 1951.

Hauck, Friedrich. *Das Evangelium des Markus.* Theologischer Handkommentar zum Neuen Testament. Leipzig: A. Diechertsche Verlagsbuchhandlung D. Wermer Scholl, 1931.

Haenchen, Ernst. *Der Weg Jesu: Eine Erklärung des Markus-Evangeliums und der kanonischen Parallelen*. Berlin: Alfred Topelmann, 1966.

Hunter, Archibald Macbride. *The Gospel According to Saint Mark*. Torch Bible Commentaries. London: SCM Press, 1949.

Johnson, Sherman E. *A Commentary on the Gospel According to St. Mark*. Black's New Testament Commentaries. London: Black, 1960.

Klostermann, Erich. *Das Markusevangelium*. Handbuch zum Neuen Testament. 4th ed. Tübingen: Mohr, 1950.

Lagrange, M.-J. *Evangile selon Saint Marc*. Etudes bibliques. 4th ed. Paris: Librairie Lecoffre, 1947.

Lohmeyer, Ernst. *Das Evangelium des Markus*. Kritisch-exegetischer Kommentar über das Neue Testament. Begründet von Heinrich August Wilhelm Meyer. 12th ed. Göttingen: Vandenhoeck & Ruprecht, 1953.

Loisy, Alfred. *L'Evangile selon Marc*. Paris: Émile Nourry, 1912.

_____. *Les Evangiles synoptiques*. Vol. I. Paris: Ceffonds, 1907.

Montefiore, Claude Goldsmid. *The Synoptic Gospels*. Vol. I: *Introduction and Gospel of Mark*. 2nd ed. New York: KTAV Publishing House, 1968.

Moule, C. F. D. *The Gospel According to Mark*. The Cambridge Bible Commentary: New English Bible. Cambridge: Cambridge University Press, 1965.

Nineham, D. E. *The Gospel of St Mark*. The Pelican New Testament Commentaries. Baltimore: Penguin Books, 1963.

Rawlinson, A. E. J. *St Mark*. Westminster Commentaries. 7th ed. London: Methuen, 1949.

Schmid, Josef. *The Gospel According to Mark*. Tr. and ed. Kevin Condon. The Regensburg New Testament. 5th ed. Staten Island, N.Y.: Alba House, 1969.

Schweizer, Eduard. *The Good News According to Mark*. Tr. Donald H. Madvig. Das Neue Testament Deutsch. Richmond, Va.: John Knox, 1970.

Swete, Henry Barclay. *The Gospel According to St Mark*. 3rd ed. New York: Macmillan, 1909.

Taylor, Vincent. *The Gospel According to St. Mark*. 2nd ed. London: Macmillan, 1966.

Wellhausen, Julius. *Das Evangelium Marci*. 2nd ed. Berlin: Georg Reimer, 1909.

D. Works on Literary Theory

Aristotle. *The "Art" of Rhetoric*. Tr. John Henry Freese. *LCL*. Cambridge: Harvard University Press, 1926.

_____. *Poetics*. Tr. W. Hamilton Fyfe. rev. ed. *LCL*. Cambridge: Harvard University Press, 1932.

Cicero. *Brutus; Orator*. Tr. H. M. Hubbell. *LCL*. Cambridge: Harvard University Press, 1962.

Holman, C. Hugh. *A Handbook to Literature*. 3rd ed. New York: Odyssey, 1972.

La Drière, James Craig. "Classification, Literary." *Dictionary of World Literary Terms*. 3rd ed. Ed. Joseph T. Shipley. Boston: The Writer, 1970.

_____. "Form." *Dictionary of World Literary Terms.* 3rd ed. Ed. Joseph T. Shipley. Boston: The Writer, 1970.

_____. "Literary Form and Form in the Other Arts." *Stil- und Formprobleme in der Literatur.* Ed. Paul Böckmann. International Federation of Modern Languages and Literatures, 7th Congress, Heidelberg, 1957. Heidelberg: Winter, 1959.

_____. "Rhetoric and 'Merely Verbal' Art." *English Institute Essays 1948.* Ed. D. A. Robertson Jr. New York: AMS Press, 1965.

_____. "Structure, Sound, and Meaning." *English Institute Essays 1956. Sound and Poetry.* Ed. Northrop Frye. New York: Columbia University Press, 1957.

Lanham, Richard A. *A Handlist of Rhetorical Terms: A Guide for Students of English Literature.* Berkeley: University of California Press, 1968.

Lausberg, Heinrich. *Handbuch der literarischen Rhetorik: Eine Grundlegung der Literaturwissenschaft.* 2 vols. Munich: Hueber, 1960.

Morier, Henri. *Dictionnaire de poétique et de rhétorique.* Paris: Presses universitaires de France, 1961.

Plato. *Euthyphro; Apology; Crito; Phaedo; Phaedrus.* Tr. Harold North Fowler. *LCL.* Cambridge: Harvard University Press, 1914.

Quintilian. *The Institutio Oratoria of Quintilian.* Tr. H. E. Butler. 4 vols. *LCL.* Cambridge: Harvard University Press, 1920-22.

Shipley, Joseph T., ed. *Dictionary of World Literary Terms.* rev., enl. ed. Boston: The Writer, 1970.

INDEX OF MODERN AUTHORS

97

INDEX OF BIBLICAL REFERENCES

98